Everything and a Kite

Everything

Ray Romano

and a Kite

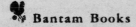

Bantam Books

New York Toronto London Sydney Auckland

Everything and a Kite

A Bantam Book

PUBLISHING HISTORY
Bantam hardcover edition / October 1998
Bantam paperback edition / September 1999

ISBN 0-553-58037-X

Published simultaneously in the United States and Canada

Bantam Books are published by Bantam Books, a division of Ran-
dom House, Inc. Its trademark, consisting of the words "Bantam
Books" and the portrayal of a rooster, is Registered in U.S. Patent
and Trademark Office and in other countries. Marca Registrada.
Bantam Books, 1540 Broadway, New York, New York 10036.

PRINTED IN THE UNITED STATES OF AMERICA

OPM   10 9 8 7 6 5 4 3 2

To my family,
who've been with me for this whole ride:

Mom and Dad
and my brothers, Richard and Robert.

And to my wife, Anna,
and kids, Alexandra, Gregory, Matthew,
and Baby Joe.

If it all goes away, I'll still have it all.

Contents

Author's Note

A lot of people were quick to give me advice about how to write my book, most of it inappropriate and some of it obscene.

But what seemed to make the most sense was what all the advice had in common: just write what you know and you'll be fine.

At first that seemed comforting. Write what I know. In a way, that's what I've been doing for the last fourteen years in my stand-up act. Writing about my observations of everyday life and my family. All I had to do was take that and translate it into a book.

Oh, if only it were that simple.

The big problem for me was that stand-up takes place in front of an audience. There's feedback. That's what you need with comedy—an audible response, so you can gauge whether something is funny or not.

In a way, comedy is like sex. The more noise you hear, the better you think you're doing.

How was I going to know what was funny without the noise?

If I was going to write a funny book, I was going to have to trust my instincts, and that scared me. My instincts and I have never seen eye to eye, and now we were going to be locked in a room together for six months.

I'll be honest, it wasn't pretty.

We yelled. We screamed.

Somebody threw a shoe.

But when it was over, we had this book.

My instincts tell me you'll like it.

Boy, I hope they're not just trying to kiss up.

Everything and a Kite

CHAPTER 1

Nimble-Minded

Immediately after I signed the contract to write this book, I got a bad feeling. The reality of what it entailed started to hit me. I mean, I loved the idea of writing a book, but as insecure and obsessive as I am, it seemed to be asking for trouble.

I had so many questions. What would it be about? What would my title be? How many chapters? Should I write it in verse?

And the typeface, the font. Good God Almighty, what about the *font*?

I didn't know from fonts. All I knew was, I had to be funny for 209 pages.

I panicked. I called the printer.

"Look, get me the funniest goddamn font you can find! I want a font where the letter 'H' looks like a clown with no pants! Get me that font!"

AFTER AN INTENSIVE SEARCH, HERE IS

THE FUNNIEST ONE I COULD FIND. OH, MAN! ARE YOU LAUGHING AS MUCH AS I AM?

I decided against that font, though I made a note of it for when I write my will.

My search continued.

For a while, I tried this one. But I think it goes a little too far in the other direction. As a matter of fact, as I'm typing this, I'm crying.

My wife tried to help.

"Choose this typeface . . . I like this one!"

No. Too girly.

But I didn't want to hurt her feelings, so I told her—and you the reader should take note of this—whenever she has dialogue in my book, it'll be in her font.

"Thank you."

You're welcome.

Still no font. It was like looking at wallpaper. None of them were quite right.

THIS WAS TOO MACHO.

This was too impersonal.

Τηισ ωασ τοο λφυτηαῶπεθ.

I think you can see I was getting desperate. I just wanted a font that felt comfortable. Like my clothes. Nothing fancy, nothing pretentious, no button fly.

So I settled on this. What you're reading right now. It fits all those qualities, and it could be funny, if I write something funny with it.

Yeah. This is my font.

Nimble-Minded

I thought the next best thing to do would be to research other books and see how they started. I shouldn't have done that, though, because after reading a few I started to get the shakes. A whole new set of worries took over.

Have you read other books? If not, I'm honored, but let me fill you in on how they work. Before you even get to Chapter One, there's a whole mess of stuff.* Introductions, Prefaces, Prologues, and whatnot.**

I think writers put all that stuff up front because they're afraid to have you dive in too fast.

They want to let you "tiptoe" into the book, like it's a cold swimming pool. Get your feet wet in the Intro, splash a little Foreword on your chest. That way, by Chapter One you're warm and comfortable, and if no one's around, you pee in it.

OK, that sounded like the right way to start. But I still had questions. How much of this preliminary stuff do you write? Can you write too much? What if it's too long, and people start peeing in the middle of my Table of Contents?

Clearly, I was troubled.

Then I remembered something that happened that made me doubt myself even more.

---

* Boy, I'll bet there's no better feeling in the world than spending twenty-two ninety-five on a book, and three pages in you're reading the phrase "whole mess of stuff." Kudos.
** See above, replacing "mess of stuff" with "whatnot."

It involved a magazine article I had recently read where a reporter described me as "nimble-minded comic Ray Romano."

OK, you ready for this? *I had to look up the word "nimble."*

Are you catching the irony in that? He was calling me smart, and yet I was too dumb to understand it.

I couldn't find a dictionary, so I tried to remember where I'd heard "nimble" before. The saddest part is, the only thing I could think of was the nursery rhyme "Jack Be Nimble, Jack Be Quick." So I did some deductive reasoning.

"Well, let's see. 'Nimble' must be related to 'quick.' It couldn't be 'Jack Be *Slow,* Jack Be Quick.' That wouldn't make sense, even I know that. So when he calls me nimble-minded, he must be giving me a compliment."

If any magazine writers are reading this and want to compliment me in the future, use words like "good."

Now, some of you may be thinking, "We've seen you on talk shows, Ray. You're not a genius, but it's not like you're a chimp."

Unfortunately, folks, talking and writing are totally different. In conversation I can feign intelligence.

"Ray, can you believe how capricious he was?"

"Yes."

Nobody's the wiser, and I can go back to my Legos.

Sometimes, I'll throw a word in a conversation even if I'm not sure it fits.

"Wow, that's incredulous!"

Then I wait, and if no one says anything, I know I got it right.

"Ray, don't you mean 'incredible'?"

Whoops.

Now I do a little dance.

"Oh, what'd I say? *'Incredulous'?* Ha! That's funny. Want to get something to eat?"

And once again here's where writing a book makes me nervous. In conversation I can do damage control. In print, if I stick an "incredulous" in there where it isn't supposed to be, my ignorance is documented for all time.

Simply put, my fear is this: a book will expose me!

I wanted to call the publisher and cancel the whole deal. So many things went through my mind.

"What if it's too late?"

"My wife already spent the advance."

"I like sand."

I was losing it again. I took a deep breath and realized I couldn't write this book if I had to worry about it revealing an ugly truth to the public. If anything, you should hear it from me directly. I have to beat my own book to the punch.

That's right, folks, the only way I can continue is to wipe the slate clean. I'm coming out of the closet.

Mom, Dad? Readers?

I'm stupid.

Damn, that felt good.

Now there's only one problem left to worry about. Since I've told you my secret, why should you be interested in reading my book at all?

I couldn't blame you if you weren't. I wouldn't read a book by a guy who's just admitted he's dumber than me.

But hear me out!

I found an angle!

And watch out, because I'm about to start nimble-ing.

Humor is usually associated with some kind of intelligence. It takes a smart person to understand the intricacies of how to make someone laugh. With the TV show and my stand-up career, I've been performing comedy for the last fourteen years.

So, in reality, what I'm doing should be marveled at. Think of what an accomplishment it is for me to be funny and also stupid.

I mean, if anything, you shouldn't feel bad about reading my book; you should feel *good*. You should be *inspired*.

Nimble-Minded

You shouldn't look at this as simply a book of funny observations, but as the work of a man who didn't let his imperfections stand in the way of his dreams.

Someday I hope to take my place among the great men of history who have done the same.

Beethoven was a great composer, yet totally deaf.

Jim Abbott pitched a no-hitter with only one arm.

Ray Romano was a comedian and thought Jell-O was a fruit.

CHAPTER 2

Mom

Folks, I want to congratulate you for getting through Chapter One.

Let's be honest. We probably lost a few.

Couple of deserters, couple of snoozers, and my father put out his cigar on page four.

We're on our way.

I guess you might be aksing* now, "What will this book actually be about?" In a nutshell: cooking and time travel.

OK, we lost a few more.

This book is by no means an autobiography. It's just observations on my life. I've tried to put them in some kind of chronological order. With that in mind, I thought I should start with the first woman I ever loved.

---

* I pronounce the word "ask" like "axed." That's how everybody in Queens pronounces it, and I'm no different. I know it's wrong, but if you want a piece of me, I'm right here. Bring it on, seriously.

Mommy!

My mother was and still is a kindly, overprotective Italian mom. Not to mention religious. Very big with the saints. She has a saint for everything.

"Mom, I'm returning these pants, they're too small."

"I'll say a prayer to Saint Bartholomew."

"There's a saint that covers *pants*?"

"If you read the Bible you'd know."

She isn't a biblical scholar, but she has her beliefs and she lives by them.

She was driving my brother Robert and me to a Little League game once and, without realizing it, accidentally cut into a funeral procession.

She got nervous. She panicked. She wanted to get out of it, but she didn't want to interrupt the sanctity of the event. Plus she thought the people behind her would follow her and get lost.

So she just kept going, trying to find the proper moment to pull out of it, until there we were, actually driving into the cemetery.

"Come on, Mom . . . I'm *pitching* today."

"We'll say a quick prayer and go."

My mother did her best to raise me to be the church-once-a-week, regular confession-going Catholic that she was.

—————

But as I grew older, I found my outlook on life changing. I've since converted to a different sect of Catholicism: *part-time* Catholicism.

Or, as we're called by the other parishioners, the "Easter-Christmas Catholics."

I'm sure you know who we are. There are many of us. And you can always spot us when we do show up in church because we're the ones who don't quite remember the moves.

When to kneel, when to stand, shake a hand, sing a song . . . we're lost. We're all just following that one old lady in the front pew.

"Kneel. She's kneeling! All right, up, get up, she's *up*! Follow her, whatever she does. Wait a minute, she's giving money, don't listen to her."

I actually grew up in a very Jewish neighborhood, Forest Hills, Queens, New York.

I loved Forest Hills. It was a great neighborhood. All my friends were Jewish, and they were great kids.

But I couldn't compete with them. And I don't mean sports.

And please . . . I don't want to sound stereotypical. I want to be politically correct. But when I say I couldn't compete, I mean that, as a kid, whenever I attempted a little kiddie business venture, I was always outdone by my Jewish friends.

We had lemonade stands every summer. There I was, all set up. I had lemonade, a box, the sign that said "5 cents" with a backwards "5." I was ready for business.

Nothing. Nothing ever sold.

Not counting the two glasses my mother would buy, I never made a dime.

Meanwhile, right across the street, there's my best friend, Murray Goldberg, open twenty-four hours a day and selling Lotto tickets.

He was *amazing*. Genius!

He wasn't even there, he had a little Korean kid working for him.

How did he *do* that?

What did I know? I was a little Italian boy. I had one angle. I offered him protection.

"That's a nice box, Murray. It'd be a shame if a Big Wheel ran it over."

Again, I hope you're taking this as just an innocent little funny story. I'm not trying to insult anyone. Yeah, sure, I stereotyped a little. But at the end I brought the jab right back around to myself, the Italian kid.

To be honest, Italian and Jewish families in my neighborhood were very similar. Especially the mothers.

The mother whose world revolved around food. Who believed any problem could be solved with food. The mother who could never accept that you were actually full.

Even now, when I visit, it's the same story. I get up from the table, put on my jacket, and start heading out, and she still won't stop. She'll wrap the food up to go.

And they're quick, these mothers. They'll beat you to the front door. They're wrap-up ninjas.

"Take it with you!"

"Mom, please . . . I'm just putting out your garbage."

"Take it anyway! Look how far away the cans are. You'll get hungry."

As far back as I can remember, she was like this. The only way I could have friends eat at my house was to brief them before they came over.

"Look. This is going to be like nothing you've ever experienced."

"Ray, don't worry, I'm really hungry. It's gonna be fine."

"Shut up, you fool! Listen to me and listen good. When you're done with the meal, if you want a little more, it's going to get very tricky. Don't tell my mother you want a little more, because then she'll serve you a whole new meal. If you want a little more, tell her you don't want *any* more. Come right out and say,

'Boy, I'm full, I couldn't eat anything else. Please, no more for me.' "

That was what you had to do. Stay one step ahead of her.

You want a little? Tell her you want *no* more.

You want a lot more? Tell her you want a little.

You don't want *any* more? You have to shoot her.

That's right, I said it! You have to shoot the woman. Or at least threaten.

Whatever you do, do it quick. Don't hesitate. As soon as you feel you've had enough to eat, just stand up and announce, "I'm done." Then pull a gun out of your vest pocket.

"Put it back in the bowl, Mrs. Romano . . . *nice and easy.* Now hand the spoon to Ray. That's it, thaaaaaat's it . . . Keep your hands where I can see them . . ."

"SHE'S GOT A CANNOLI IN HER APRON!"

Shoot her! You have to shoot her. And land one. Don't graze her, that'll just piss her off.

She'll take a bullet and keep coming. There's no quit in her. She won't just go down, she'll pass the food off to my aunt. There's always a fat aunt backing her up.

"Take this, Maria—he's a runner! Feed him without me!"

·   ·   ·

Of course, the upside to Mom's obsession was the amount of food I would get to take to school in my lunch bag. I brought a lot to the table when it came to the old grammar school lunch trading market. I had quantity, I had quality, and to top it off, I had Murray Goldberg as my broker.

"Ray, for half that chicken parmesan, I can get you a tuna salad, a Yoo-Hoo, and an ice cream to be named later. But we gotta go *now*."*

I used to love the bag lunch. And Mom knew she did a good job. She was proud of her work, and it never wavered. It was always the same size brown bag, top folded down three times, and it wasn't complete until she whipped out the Magic Marker and wrote, on both sides of the bag:

RAY

Everybody knew whose lunch that was.

It didn't stop at school, either. I lived at home until I was twenty-nine, doing many different things. I was a college student, a bank teller, a truck driver. Through it all, the one constant was Mom's bag lunch.

Boy, I loved that lunch.

When my mother reads this, I'm sure she'll be flattered, but she'll probably scold me for mentioning that

---

* Italian women have mustaches. OK, we're even.

I was a truck driver. She thinks that if people know I worked a blue-collar job, they'll assume I'm uneducated.

"Why don't you ever tell the people how you studied accounting?"

Look, I drove a mattress truck in Manhattan, and I'm proud of it. I was a good truck driver. Never got a moving violation.

I did come close once. A police officer pulled me over. I guess he thought the light was red, I thought it was yellow, who's to say? As he walked toward my truck, I reached for my license and realized that I had left my wallet at home.

I remained fairly calm and explained to him my situation. No wallet.

It was when he got this indignant look on his face that my imagination got the best of me. All I could think of was where was I going to hide a paper clip on my body so I could jimmy the handcuffs open like they do in those prison movies.

I started sweating a little, and he said, "Listen, sir, I need some kind of identification. I don't know who you are."

And it was a reflex. I wasn't trying to be funny. But with one motion I grabbed my bag lunch and held it up to his face.

"I'm

RAY!"

Showed him the other side.

RAY

I didn't get a ticket. I'm not going to explain further. All you need to know is that for the rest of the day that officer's breath smelled like chicken parmesan.

I lived in the typical Italian home.

The plastic furniture you couldn't sit on. Bathroom towels you weren't allowed to touch. China that no one's ever going to use.

It was a museum.

Everything in my mother's house is for a special occasion that hasn't happened *yet*.

My mother's waiting for the Pope to show up for dinner to break out the good stuff. Or Tony Danza.

Growing up, I had to attend thousands of Italian social events. These included the dreaded Italian wedding. Now, as a little kid, this wasn't so bad. Lots of

food, and usually you could give the adults the slip and
go break something.

But today I get the shivers when my wife and I are
invited to one. I'm not antisocial. But I do have a few
simple gripes against those big Italian weddings.

For starters, if I have to chicken-dance again, I'm
going to kill somebody.

Listen, I'm not against *dancing* at weddings. It's a
celebration, and of course people should dance if they
want to.

But what's the reason it's always got to be a *stupid*
dance? The Chicken. The Hokey-Pokey. The Slide.
And my personal dance enemy, The Train.

I'm always getting sucked into that conga line of
idiots. They sneak up on you. They blindside you. You
don't even see them coming. You get up from your
chair, take two steps, next thing you know, some
stranger's got his hands around your hips.

"No, no . . . I'm just going to the men's
room . . . no, no . . . ohhhhhhh, come on!"

You're in. It's over. Forget it. You better have a
strong bladder, because you're going to be cha-cha-ing
until the song is done. Sometimes until the end of the
reception. There's no getting away. You can't disen-
gage. You let go of the guy in front of you and try to
walk away, and now you're the conductor for whoever
is attached to you.

Now there's *two* trains shimmying around the room.

The train is like an earthworm: cut it in half and both sides are still moving. Your only hope is to try to run them into each other.

Otherwise they're going to hang on and follow you right into the men's room.

"Hey, where's the train leader taking us? What's he doing? Wait, he stopped, the train stopped. Oh . . . um . . . *shake*, everybody, he's *shaking*!"

Of course, the only thing that bothers me more than dancing at a wedding is my *mother* dancing at a wedding.

And let me tell you something. I know there are many ways to describe your emotions, but I think as a people we need to come up with another one for what you feel when you see your mother do The Electric Slide. We don't have a word for it yet, but it's a combination of shame, panic, revulsion, and, oddly enough, pride.

Could someone please name that? How about "plunkish"? As in, "Honey, your mom's dancing. Now, don't get all *plunkish* on us."

Of course, now that I live 2,500 miles away, I miss Mom. I miss the worrying, the meals, the Vicks

VapoRub. I even miss the way she never quite learned how to use the VCR.

Oh, our VCR. She was actually afraid of it. VCRs were like Kryptonite to my mother. Whenever she was yelling at me for something, I'd just pick it up and scare her out of the room.

"Back it up, Ma . . . look what I got!"

I can laugh now, but I can't tell you how frustrating it was when I had to call her up on the phone because I left the house without setting the VCR.

"Listen, Ma, the game's on, and I need you to set the VCR for me. What? . . . No, you don't need your rosary beads! It'll be all right. I'll talk you through it. Look at the button on the left. What's it say? . . . 'Snooze alarm'? OK, go downstairs, Ma."

Don't worry, I still talk to her on the phone a couple times a week. But let me say this about using the telephone to keep in touch with your mother:

America, can we please find a better system?

You know what I'm talking about. Once a mother reaches a certain age, there's something about the phone that makes her forget that time exists at all.

Don't get me wrong. I'm a good son. I don't mind talking with Mom, even though my half of the conversation is a half hour of "uh-huh" and the occasional "you don't say." (For those of you in the South, that's "reckon so" and "y'all are kiddin'.")

But how do you politely end it? That's the problem. Again, I love talking to her, but what the world needs is some kind of nice way to let someone know that it's time to end a phone call.

And I may have figured something out.

Last year I cohosted the People's Choice Awards. I'm not bragging, but let's just say I got to meet Regis Philbin.

Stay with me.

All the award recipients had an allotment of forty-five seconds to make an acceptance speech. Now, I'm sure you've seen what I'm about to describe on an awards show at one time or another.

If a person went over their time, the band would start to play a little something in the background. Nothing loud, usually just some tinkling on the piano to let them know it was time to wrap things up. The speaker would hastily finish his speech and leave the stage.

Bingooooooooo!

There it is! AT&T, wake up and smell your redial!

How great would that be? Right there, next to "mute" and "flash."

The "wrap-it-up" button.

You're talking to Mom. It's getting late.

". . . sounds like a great buffet . . . uh-huh . . . you don't say . . . yes, Mom, I've had big shrimp."

One push of a button: *Tinkle, tinkle . . .*

"Oh, they're playing you off, Mom."

"Oh, OK. Well, I know I'm going to forget people, but I want to thank everyone involved, especially your dad, who drove me to the wedding in the first place. Love you, bye. Put on a sweater!"

Click.

Phone companies, please get this feature.

I don't want to have to buy a piano.

CHAPTER 3

Dad

I've always said that if my father had hugged me once, I would never be in show business.

My theory has always been that everyone in show business is there because they were deprived of some attention as a child.

Every performer. Every singer, every dancer, every movie and TV star. If these people got their required attention as a child, there'd be no entertainers at all. Nothing for us to sing, watch, or read.

Thank God for undemonstrative parents, or we'd all be bowling.

On the upside, there'd be no karaoke.

To be fair to my father, he did hug me once on my twenty-first birthday. It was very awkward, and I think I know what it was that made me feel so uncomfortable.

The nudity.

Whoa, folks. Little jokey-poo there. Easy does it.

Calm down. Come on back. Once in a while I'm going to throw one in there just to see if you're paying attention.

To be honest, my father is probably the person that I got my sense of humor from. I'm not saying I got *his* sense of humor. I'm saying I got *a* sense of humor.

His sense of humor I don't think anybody has. I can't quite describe it. He's got a very bizarre, dry way of *trying* to be funny, a very slow, droll manner of speaking, so it's hard to detect that he's joking at all. Very subtle.

And it's dangerous, because if you don't know he's trying to be funny, you could take him the wrong way.

Unfortunately, to this day my wife is taking him the wrong way.

I'm kind of stuck in the middle. I can't tell you how many times I've tried to calm my wife down with the same pleas.

"He's *joking*! He's making a *joke*!"

"Well, I'm sorry! I don't see how it's funny when he says he thinks one of our two-year-old twins has 'homosexual tendencies.' "

True story.*

---

* The fact that I put "true story" here doesn't mean that everything else you've read *isn't* true. It's *all* true, but I'm just afraid some of the things my father does you're gonna think I made up. I didn't. Hold me.

I've tried to explain my father's sense of humor to my wife countless times, but she just doesn't get him.

The dangerous thing is, I find him funny. I'm not condoning his actions. Look, he's a pain in the ass to me too. But even though he drives my wife crazy, I have to laugh sometimes. Quietly. To myself.

Of course, his comic masterpiece—or as we refer to it, the "Answering Machine Incident"—almost broke up our marriage.

Don't get me wrong. The Answering Machine Incident was not without comedic merit. The timing was bad, though; my wife was still alive.

My dad figured out—I don't know how, I don't know why—how to call into our answering machine and retrieve our messages. He cracked our answering machine code.

He'd listen to our messages, then call back and leave us a message advising us what to do about the *other* messages.

"Ray, the guy from the gas station called, your car's gonna be ready tomorrow. What'd you do to it? I told you to check the oil, ya dummy. And why did Anna's gyno call? Is she pregnant again?"

Three, two, one . . .

"What the hell is he doing? That's like reading our mail, Ray. Don't tell me you think this is funny."

I thought it was kind of funny.

I talked her down, she got over it, life returned to normal.

Until the next day, when my father figured out how to change our *outgoing* message. My wife and I were at a friend's house and we called our machine. Instead of hearing my voice on the outgoing message, we heard my father's.

"Uh, hi . . . ! You've reached Ray and Anna. If you want them, leave a message at the beep. If you want me, Al Romano, I'm at 555-2006."

I want to thank my father, because without him I would never have had the pleasure of hearing my wife say the word "cocksucker."

I don't want to paint the wrong picture of my father. His pranks may sound mean-spirited, but let me tell you something. I grew up with him, and believe me, it's a lot better now than forty years ago when he was, shall we say, *prankless*.

Back then, all I remember is him being a guy who had a little bit of a temper. Certain things would just set him off.

One place I never wanted to be with my father was in the car while he was driving, stuck in traffic. I know no one likes traffic and we're all frustrated when we're in it, but my dad had a particularly low tolerance for people when he was on the road.

Everyone around us became a "hump."

"Look at this hump, tryin' to squeeze in on me. I see ya! You're not going anywhere, ya *hump*."

My mother would always try to contain his anger. "Albert, please, you're scaring the children. Just calm down . . . and let the fire truck go by."

"Fire my *ass*! It's lunchtime for these humps! There's always a fire at lunchtime, right? Go ahead, ya hump!"

One time when I was older I made the mistake of actually saying something to him while he was in "hump" mode.

"Dad, you're right on this guy's bumper. Pull back a little."

"Ohhhhh . . . look at Mr. Know-It-All! Mr. College Boy. Mr. Philosophy Major. Hey, why don't you go back to school and waste another twenty thousand dollars of my life with that 'tree falls in the forest' *bullcrap*. 'I hump, therefore I am,' okay? Or how about this: 'I hump, therefore *you* am.' How's that sound, Socrates?"

"All right, Dad, relax."

Wherever we had to be, we were usually late because he was always implementing some plan or theory to avoid the traffic.

"If we leave now it'll be rush hour and it'll take an hour to get there. But if we leave in a half hour, they'll be no traffic and it'll only take fifteen minutes to get there. We'll actually pass ourselves had we left right now."

My father was the disciplinarian of the house. He didn't go overboard, but he was from the old school, and if we did something wrong, he wasn't above a little smack on the butt.

I remember once when I was about nine, I was riding bikes with my brother Richard, and I almost got hit by a car. I wasn't looking, but luckily the car stopped short and the only thing that got scratched was my bike.

On our way home, Richard said he was going to tell my father what happened unless I gave him a dime.

Now, like I say, Dad was the discipline guy, so this kind of "gimme a dime" blackmail went on all the time between me and my brothers. You didn't want Dad to find out if you screwed up in any way.

"I'll give you a nickel."

"No. A dime."

"No, no way. What did I do wrong? I'll give you a nickel."

"Sorry, a dime or nothing."

"Then nothing . . . idiot."

"Dickhead."

"Pimpleface."

OK, you get the picture. We called each other

names for the whole ride home, and needless to say, we never struck a deal.

When we got in the house, my brother told my dad. Guess what happened?

Let's just say that would have been a dime well spent.

On its face, there seems to be no logic getting a spanking for almost being hit by a car. What was my dad thinking? "Thank God you're not hurt, so *I* can hurt you."

But now that I'm a parent, I understand where that comes from. When your kids do something careless that puts them in danger, it scares you so much, you want to teach them a lesson so they'll never do it again.

The weird part is, if I had been even slightly hurt by the car, I would never have gotten the spanking.

So, basically, one of two things could have happened:

1) The car hits me, I get hurt.

2) The car misses me, I get spanked.

Obviously, the moral to the story is "Don't lowball."

Ironically, lowballing was my father's specialty. He was a man obsessed with haggling. As I got older, whenever I paid for something, he'd always ask how much it cost, and I'd be afraid to tell him because I knew what was coming next.

"Forty dollars for that haircut? Holy Christ, you're dumber than I tell people."

When I started doing stand-up and making money, he'd always ask how much I made on every gig. It was never enough.

"That's it? That's all they gave you?"

"That's it, Dad."

"Well, can you Screw the Uncle at least?"

Let me explain "Screw the Uncle."

One of the things my father hated most—and when you're talking about things my father hated, it's a very long list—was the government. To be more specific, having to pay the government.

"They want a piece of everything you got! Bastards. You pick your nose and find a dime in there, they want some of it!"

So Screwing the Uncle—the "Uncle" being Uncle Sam—was his way of asking if I didn't have to pay taxes. That he loved.

"Can you Screw the Uncle with the money?"

"Yeah, Dad. It's off the books."

"Atta boy."

As I explained in the previous chapter, now that I've moved to Los Angeles, I keep in contact with my parents about twice a week on the phone. But Dad's phone personality is quite the opposite of Mom's.

While my mother never lacks for something to say, when my father gets on, it's always a little awkward. Like I said, he isn't a very demonstrative guy. And probably because of that, I tend to be the same way.

We never really know what to say to each other. Sports is about the only thing we can talk about comfortably. We have that in common. So he kind of rushes through the required topics, just to get to sports.

"How are the kids?"

"Fine."

"Anna?"

"Fine."

"You?"

"Fine."

"Fuckin' Yankees!"

"Tell me about it!"

And we both relax.

Actually, now that I have a TV show, we talk a little bit more. He's taken an interest.

"Hey, I saw you beat *Cosby* last week in the ratings."

"Yeah, Dad, by a little."

"So they should pay you more than they pay him."

"That's not how it works, Dad."

It's very strange to see what he has to say about my television world. He's got a sharp business mind, but he knows nothing about show business. We're talking about a man whose last movie he saw in a theater was *Patton*.

It makes for interesting conversation. There was one week where CBS had a college basketball game that ended about a half hour early. So they ran one of our episodes to fill the time. The next day I got a call from Dad.

"Hey, Raymond? You know they ran one of your shows yesterday after the game?"

"Yeah, I know."

"They gotta pay you for that."

"They will, Dad."

My father thinks if I don't call CBS every time my show airs, I don't get paid.

"Hello, CBS? This is Ray Romano. Yeah, my dad just told me you ran one of my episodes last night."

"Oh, he did? Well, you caught us! We'll send a check right out to you. Listen, we need a one-hour rerun for tomorrow night, but we don't want to pay anyone. Do you know if Chuck Norris is out of the country?"

·   ·   ·

I make more money now than I used to, and last Christmas I went out and bought my parents a brand-new car.

It felt good. It was the first time in his life my dad owned a brand-new automobile. He was always good with cars, and he could fix almost anything on them. Which was fine. Although combine that with being a little frugal, and you have a guy who would never have thought he had to spend more for a car than I would for a haircut.

The car I remember most was a 1964 Falcon, which my father bought from some guy in 1974 for fifty dollars. He fixed it all up, and we had it until 1984. That's from when I was seventeen until I was twenty-seven.

Let me explain the ramifications of that. Seventeen to twenty-seven are your prime dating years. And as far as women go, they were enough of a challenge for me to begin with.

Now, throw a '64 Falcon into the mix. Do you need any more explanation, or should I show you the prom pictures with my cousin?

So Christmastime I give Mom and Dad a brand-new car. Should be a good thing, right? Seems logical.

Before: only old cars.

Now: *new* car!

Before: always pay for car.

Now: *free* car!

Everyone should be happy, right? And for one golden moment, when we gave it to them, everyone was. My mother cried, my father actually smiled. Everything was perfect. And then:

"Will I know how to drive it? It's brand-new."

"Oh Christ, what's the insurance on that?"

"I heard those airbags are dangerous."

"What made you think I like green?"

And so went Christmas Day.

The next morning, before we left for the airport, I peeked out the back window and saw an image that left a warm Hallmark feeling in my heart. There were my mom and dad, sitting in the front seat of the car, which was in the garage, with the wipers on.

Faintly I could hear them yelling.

"Albert, teach me about the intermittent."

"Read the goddamn manual."

Last time I talked to my father on the phone, I got very annoyed at him because it's been six months and the car still has its original tank of gas.

"Why don't you use it?"

"I don't want to run it into the ground. I want it to last."

"Dad, you're seventy-three, and Mom's seventy. What are you waiting for?"

"What does our age gotta do with it?"

"I'm just saying, you're seventy-three."

"Yeah?"

"I don't know. I'm just saying you're getting kinda . . ."

"What?"

"You know, I mean, just how long do you, uh . . ."

"What, what? Spit it out!"

". . . Fuckin' Yankees, huh?"

CHAPTER 4

Single Guy

People think living in your parents' basement until you're twenty-nine is lame. But what they don't realize is that while you're there you save money on rent, food, and dates.

Wow, did I save money on dates.

The line "Hey, what do you say we go to a movie and then hang out in my parents' basement?" only works if you and your date are fifteen. Or if she really likes mold.

It was hard to treat the place as a bachelor pad. Normally, when you have a woman over to your apartment, the first thing you do is give her the grand tour, show off all your cool stuff. The nicest thing in my place was the hot water heater.

I still tried to make it sound impressive. "Yep. This is where it all happens. Someone takes a shower in this house, they gotta go through me."

Me have no sex back then.

I remember the first time my wife (then girlfriend) came over to the basement. I spent the entire day cleaning it, just so I could say, "Sorry the place is such a mess."

I had to clean all day to qualify for mess status.

The truth is, what really kept me from dating was my fear of rejection, a fear that still remains strong today.

Of course, after I got married, I no longer had to worry about dating. But the fear of rejection didn't subside, it mutated. It franchised itself into many aspects of my life.

I now can find rejection in any situation. I am a rejection archeologist.

My feelings can get hurt trying to buy a can of soda. Look, I know, logically, a soda machine has nothing against me. I know that when it spits back my dollar, it's not personal. I shouldn't feel bad. I should just reach back in my wallet and try another dollar.

But it hurts me.

It may seem silly, but when my dollar comes crawling back out of that machine, I feel inadequate.

And it's not like I don't check the dollar. I'm not just reaching in blind and pulling any old ragged bill out of my pocket. I get a good one. I check the corners. I make sure that dollar is soda-ready.

And with cautious optimism I put it into the machine. Now, here's the cruel part: it takes it a little! It teases you. The machine is taking in your dollar, and you start to get psyched.

"I've been approved for soda . . ."

Suddenly you're making friends with strangers.

"You thirsty, Skinny? I got soda coming."

Soda's on the way, and all is right with the world.

Then something in the air changes. Everything's in slow motion. A strange *whrr* from the machine. My dollar has suddenly stopped. A clap of thunder. I look over at Skinny and he's laughing at me. And then, with a sickening whine, my dollar is regurgitated.

No soda for you, loser.

Usually, then, I just black out.

All right, maybe I'm being a little dramatic. But you have to understand, when I see that dollar come back, it's quite a frustrating experience.

Because at first you don't accept what's happened. You shimmy the dollar back and forth on the corner of the machine to flatten it out. Or you try to jam it back in quickly, like you'll catch the machine off guard.

None of it works. Then you enter the denial stage. You try it face down, even though the instructions say face up.

Right back out it comes. No amount of coaxing is getting that dollar in past the soda machine bouncer.

"Hey, I'm not gonna tell you again, Wrinkly. It's *over*."

• • •

So if I can be that affected by an inanimate object, you can imagine my fear of interacting with humans. More specifically, the opposite sex.

I'm not the smoothest around women. Even now, when there's no dating tension involved, I get flustered just trying to say hello.

Saying hello to a woman has always been a problem for me. Let's say you're at a party, and you see a woman who's an acquaintance, and she's approaching. What do you do? How do you greet her? Is it a handshake? Or is it that little "cheek-kiss"?

It's a very tough call. First off, shaking hands with a woman is always a little weird to me. It seems too formal. It's almost as if you're afraid of being too physical.

Whenever I shake a woman's hand, I always think she's interpreting it as my saying, "You're very attractive, and if I touch you any more than this, I might have an accident."

On the other hand, the cheek-kiss has its own set of problems. First of all, you definitely can't assume that a cheek-kiss is a given. If there was a precedent set, like you met her at a party some other time and she initiated a cheek-kiss, then you're all set. That's a no-brainer.

But I have a hard enough time just trying to remember people's names, much less their preferred method of greeting. What I do is have my wife, who's very good with names and faces, stand right behind me when we go to parties, and coach.

"Incoming, 12:00. Name's Betty, cheek-kiss, and ask her how her father's feeling."

It's when I'm alone and there's no precedent on file that I'm in trouble.

My method is to say hello, and then lean the head in just a little. Not too much, but just enough to see if she responds.

Be careful, though. You don't want to lean in too far because then you're committed. That's one of the worst feelings in the world, to be mid-cheek-kiss-lean-in and see her hand come up for a handshake. Then it's like Mayday in your head.

"Grab her hand and kiss *that*!"

"Pretend you're falling!"

"Punch her!"

When you're caught in that situation, what I find works is to keep leaning in and whisper something in her ear, like that was your plan all along.

"The potato chips are stale. Pass it on."

Married or single, when it comes to women, I'm a doof.

Which is why, when a bunch of my friends are sitting around talking and the conversation, as it inevitably does, turns to past sexual escapades, I always get snacks.

I don't have much to contribute to that discussion. And the question will always come up: "How many?" The old "how many" question. What blows my mind every time is when some guy's asked how many, and his first response is "Let me see . . ."

Let me see?

What the hell is he saying "let me see" for? "Let me see" is something you say when somebody asks you to try and name all the presidents.

But "let me see" in response to the "how many" question?

Right there I know I'm in over my head. I don't need time to search the memory banks. It's a very simple number. I wear it on my softball uniform.

Now, I'm not going to come right out and tell you what it is. I don't think you need to know. But look, you bought my book, so if it's of interest to you, here's a hint: my "how many" number happens to be one less than the number of times I've been stung by a bee.

Does that help you at all? Think about how many times you've been stung by a bee. Unless you're a bee-keeper, you're probably laughing at me. Well, stop.

Honestly, I don't care. As a matter of fact, in today's immoral society I think I'm refreshing. At least that's what I tell myself to stop the crying.

Hey, if you want to play this game a little more, I'm

in. You don't scare me. Here. Knock yourself out, tough guy.

My "how many" number is also *less* than the number of times I've thrown up. There you go. I'm standing right here. Want another?

I've been to a *bris* more times than my "how many" number. OK?

Now, don't get all full of yourself. Papa Bear did have a little honey. Matter of fact, try this on.

My "how many" number is *greater* than the number of times I've put a pet to sleep. So there you go. You kind of know where I stand, and I've still managed to keep a little air of mystery about the whole thing.

And you know what? Why the hell not throw in a little bonus round.

My "how many" number is *exactly equal* to the number of times I've been crapped on by a bird.*

I've said enough.

Of course, now that I'm married with kids, I've reached a whole other not-having-sex dynamic. The opportunity is always there, but the motivation is sometimes lacking.

---

* Play along and prove a little theory of mine. See how long it takes you to remember where you were during one of the greatest accomplishments in history: man walking on the moon.

Now do the same thing for where you were when a bird crapped on you.

See what I'm saying?

That's not just me, it's my wife too. We want to be in the mood, it's just so hard to get there after a long day of work and the kids.

Of course, my single friends are quick to offer their cures.

"You know what you do? Go to the adult section of the video store and pick out one of those movies."

Nope. First of all, it's hard to find the time to do that with all the kids around. And even once they're all asleep, it's tough to stay in the mood to watch one of those movies when you have to go to the VCR and eject *Thumbelina*.

Another bit of advice I hear is:

"Ray, why don't you and her just get a babysitter and go to a motel room?"

Once again, shut up, single friend.

Those motels make very little sense when you're married. First of all, you're giving up one of the big perks of marriage, which is not having to pay any expenses for sex.

Secondly, when you go to one, they charge you for a minimum of four hours.

Four hours! Now, come on. And this question goes out to all men: Who needs a room for *four hours*?

If we ever did go to one of those places, I'd go right to the front desk and lay it on the line.

"I want a twenty-minute room. That's right, a twenty-minute room! And it's gotta have a TV. Don't look at me funny—we're married! Do you have a drive-thru? Because we both know what we want."

Look, even when I was single, four hours was an unrealistic fantasy. Oh sure, it's a goal. You start out with high hopes. In your head you talk a good game.

"Oh man, they should put a number on my back right now, because this is gonna be a *marathon*. I'm gonna need someone to bring me cups of water in the middle of this. I should get sponsors."

But it never turns out that way. As soon as you're out of the blocks, your marathon dreams are over and you go right to the scorer's table to transfer yourself into the hundred-yard dash.

That's the problem. You don't have enough discipline to pace yourself. You think you're staying within your boundaries, but you always end up going that one move *too far*.

That's what gets you every time. That one move. It's always the one move. Of course, you make a futile attempt to try and save the whole thing.

"Honey, freeze! Don't do anything—don't BREATHE! Ohhhhhhhh . . . you *moved*. It's not my fault. You clearly exhaled."

Don't tell me four hours.

If a guy's ever telling you a four-hour sex story with a straight face, just feel sorry for him. Not for lying to you, but for lying to himself. As a matter of fact, stop him right in the middle of the story and just hug him. Nine times out of ten he'll just break down and cry.

He knows you know.

That's the problem with men. We like to brag. And it all comes from the same place: insecurity. Men feel the need to constantly protect the macho image.

That's why if you gave the guy telling you a four-hour sex story a hug, it would throw his whole macho equilibrium out of whack. He'd have to add in details about how, after the sex, he ran outside and wrestled a bobcat.

Men have all got that "don't get too physically close to another man" mentality.

You ever watch a man when he's holding a door open for a woman and then a man behind her is trying to get through on that same hold?

Oh no. Oh, no no *no*. You can't hold the door for another guy.

"Look, I'm doing this for *her*, pal. Don't think you can just sashay in here on my dime."

When it comes to holding the door, the most a man will do for another man is get him started. If he sees you coming, he's going to start to walk away, but before he does, he'll give the door a little "there ya go" flip.

Even then he might feel like he has to go home and shower.

We don't want to get too close.

Of course, ground zero for this paranoia is the public men's room.

Women think it's all a big locker room mentality in there, like we're all snapping each other's asses with towels and spitting on each other. But truth be told, no man likes to share a bathroom with other guys.

When a man walks into a men's room and takes his place at a crowded string of urinals, there's just too much pressure. So many things to worry about.

What if I'm too nervous to pee?

What if I don't pee long *enough*?

What if I pee too long?

What if I'm peeing and I make a sound in the middle?

And God forbid, what if I accidentally glance at another man's genitals?

And double God forbid, what if he catches me?

And Final Jeopardy God forbid, what if he catches me *because he was glancing at my genitals?*

See? That's what goes on in there, ladies. It's no party.

And if you've ever wished you were a fly on a men's

room wall so you could hear what we're saying, you're wasting your time. It's no yap fest, either.

We don't want to talk, we don't want to look, and we don't want to touch. To most guys, the ideal public men's room would be a sensory deprivation tank that flushes.

The most uncomfortable men's room arrangement is "the trough," which is still popular at old bars and large sports stadiums.

For you ladies who don't know what I'm talking about, imagine one giant urinal, about the size of a long bathtub. No little miniwalls in between you, no partitions of any kind.

Just a full-bore, no-holds-barred, man-next-to-man-hey-watch-where-you're-spraying pee fest.

Oh, it's humiliating. Everyone's violating airspace, you're catching all kinds of bounce-back . . . you don't even get your own little chunk of ice or one of those plastic strainer things to use as a target. Everybody just pulls out their equipment and starts flooding the area, like you're trying to put out a four-alarm fire in Tiny Town.

Let me tell you: if women have anything like that in their bathrooms, I don't want to know about it.*

---

* All right, send me some pictures.

CHAPTER 5

Married Guy

I got married when I was twenty-nine. Up until that time I was still living at home.

So I went—overnight—from living alone in a room in my parents' basement to sharing an entire house with a woman.

(Whimper sound.)

As time has gone by, I've adapted pretty well. But having no experience living under the same roof with a person of the opposite sex, I learned the hard way how crucial that first day together is.

There are choices you make on day one that don't seem important, but oh . . . they are.

What side of the bed do you want?

That seemed trivial at the time. How important could that be? Well, if there are any soon-to-be-married men reading this, listen to me . . .

THAT'S YOUR SIDE FOR LIFE!!

Think it over, Romeo, because I blew the call. I got

47

screwed. I didn't stop to consider any of the important factors—the phone access, bathroom proximity, or the mother of them all: *TV angle*.

Please, if I can relay any message in this book, it's side-of-the-bed-choosing awareness. Don't end up like me. For the rest of my life I have to watch TV with my wife's big toe in the middle of the screen.

Do you hear what I'm saying? When I watch the weather report, all I get is from Wednesday over.

Please, think about it! You need to consider all the variables. I didn't. I never thought it would matter. The only thing that even occurred to me was a child-hood instinct. I took the side of the bed that was away from the door, in case the bogeyman came in. That's the only thing I factored in.

"OK, let's see, the bogeyman gets her . . . and . . . I'll be in my spaceship by then . . ."

The choice is yours.

Along with side of the bed, another very important decision is *size* of the bed.

We started out with a queen-size and have since graduated to a king. I can't tell you how much better it is with that extra space. The only downside is that I'm so used to it now, I can't sleep with my wife in anything else.

If we're in a hotel that only has a queen, I'm

screwed. It's like going from first class down to coach. We're both amazed that this is the way we used to live.

"How did I ever sleep with your ass in my back?"

"I don't know, Freezer Feet."

I've been in hotels where they don't even have a queen, and they expect two people to sleep in a sorry little cot they call the double bed.

"Double" is the most misleading label in the mattress world. I don't know what it pertains to, but it definitely can't be the size. Maybe it's the fact that after you sleep in one with your wife, there's double the chance you'll get divorced the next day.

On the other hand, it's clear why they call it a king-size bed. Because when you're in it, YOU ARE THE KING! You're in your own little country over there on your side. It's your empire to rule. You make little decrees about what food is allowed, what books can stay on the night table. Once in a while you execute a toenail.

Over on her side, who knows what the hell is going on? It's a land of mystery. All you really know for sure is the whole place smells like moisturizer.

The only real benefit in getting a smaller bed is that you get credit for cuddling, whether intentional or not. You're not going to get away with that in a big bed. No, no. Once you've gone king, cuddling requires a conscious effort.

You can't just move your leg, do a little rubbing,

and call it a night. First of all, you've got to get over there. Even the kiss good night requires rolling over a couple of times.

Usually we agree to meet in the middle. Of course, when I want to seduce her, I'll make the whole trip myself. But by the time I get there, I'm sweating, I'm breathing heavy, and she thinks I started without her.

Even so, the pluses of the king far outweigh the minuses. Especially if you have kids. Once they start climbing in with you during the night, you better have a big bed or you're going to wake up every morning with a mouthful of toes.

I think I've made it clear: for the sake of your marriage, get a king-size bed.

And if you really want to stay married, get *two*.

OK, men. That's it for the bed advice. Let's move on to chores and duties.

Don't make that face.

Just accept that certain duties will be assigned to you.

I know you know about most of them. They're traditional: taking out the garbage, mowing the lawn. But there's more. There are many other lesser-known ones that are just as important.

For starters, right after we moved in together, I

found out that in the middle of the night I was the automatic *noise checker-outer*.

Any little thing she heard.

"What's that?"

"Nothing. Go to sleep. It's nothing."

"No, no, <u>check it out</u>! I can't sleep! It could be a burglar. He might have a gun . . . so . . . go!"

"Oh, come on. Really?"

"Yes! I heard something. I think we're being robbed. Now go. And be careful. Put your slippers on."

"OK, thanks."

"Just shut up and go."

"I'm going."

"Bring me up a yogurt if it's nothing."

"OK."

"Either way. I want a yogurt either way. Don't come back without a yogurt."

The sad part is, you have to go. You are the noise checker-outer. Whether you're qualified or not, you are *it*. It's like ascending to the throne in a monarchy. You could be a moron, but if you're next in line, you're the new leader.

I accept it. I'm the noise checker.

Now, don't get the impression that I'm this big macho hero. If I hear a noise, my first instinct is to run, hide, cry, and then itch.

But I don't. I do my duty. The way I figure it, it's the least I can do in the relationship. She has to dress me for functions, be nice to my parents, and occasionally squeeze another person out of her body. I have to check out a noise.

We're even.

Of course, after a few noise-checking episodes, you realize you need to select some makeshift weapon that you will keep under your bed.

Most often it's a bat or bat-type object. A monkey wrench, a golf club . . . there's no real rule of thumb, except that I would avoid using any member of the Wiffle family. You're not going to scare anybody with something that whistles when you swing it.

Over the years I've taken to calling this the "Who's Down There?" weapon.

Because that's the chain of events:

Noise.

Elbow from wife.

Grab weapon.

"Who's down there?"

Silence.

Back to bed.

"Sex?"

"No."

Snore.

·   ·   ·

Again, any members of the Hide and Itch club like myself out there, don't be misled. Just because you have a weapon doesn't mean you're ever going to use it.

"Who's down there?"

"My name's Rocky and I'm taking some of your things."

"Um . . . could you throw me up a yogurt?"

Along with noise checker-outer comes the job of *bug killer*. And once again, I don't know why this is automatically given to the man. Why do women assume men aren't squeamish? I'm not a bug man. I'm secure enough to admit to being afraid of bugs. But men really have no choice. Bugs are simply our jurisdiction.

The other day my wife screamed from the bathroom. It was quick and sharp, and I recognized it immediately as her "bug" scream. I was downstairs on the couch, and just waited.

There was silence, which was strange. Usually after the bug scream, there's another.

"Ray!"

There it is. Then I usually pretend not to hear that and hope she'll handle it herself.

"RAY!"

Yeah, she never does.

I ran up to the bathroom and there by the tub was this huge, monstrous bug. It was gigantic. It fright-

ened me. It was ugly, it had a lot of twisty-curly
things, it was gross.

And we have a clean bathroom, OK?

(My wife wrote that.)

But this bug was very nasty, and my wife was hysterical.

**"Kill it. What are you looking at it for? Get in there and
kill it!"**

Right. Look, even if you're not scared of bugs, there
are some bugs that you just don't rush in and kill. You
have to plan it out. Do a couple of dry runs in your
head. A lot of things could go wrong. What if you
swing and miss? You don't know if he has the gift of
flight.

That's all I pictured. That ugly bug: mad, airborne,
and headed for my nostrils.

Then she told me to spray him.

Some women think that any aerosol can kill a bug.
Anything that sprays.

"Deodorant! Use that! I've killed bugs with deodorant!!"

Try that. Try killing a monster with deodorant. It's
not easy. And all I could find was the roll-on.

"This isn't working. He likes this . . . What do
you mean, how do I know? He's purring."

Of course, scarier than bug killing and noise checking was the day I was actually sent out to do the chore
of . . . (nervous swallow) food shopping.

(Whimper sound. Slight gas leak?)

Married Guy

Let me tell you something about food shopping. I don't do it. And I'm not a chauvinist. I'm not sexist. I just don't know *how* to do it. I came from an Italian house. The refrigerator was always full. I never knew you had to buy food. I thought there were food fairies that came at night.

I'll never forget the day my wife sent me to the supermarket. Bad enough I didn't know what I was doing. She also gave me—are you ready for this?—a handful of *coupons*.

Ladies, ladies, ladies! Please don't ever give a man coupons. We can't handle that. Men are too insecure for coupons. I don't care what kind of Renaissance man you think you're married to, no man is going to look a speedy register girl right in her eye just to claim he's got twenty cents off the Cocoa Pebbles.

"Slow it down there, Fast Fingers. I got plenty more right here in my fanny pack."

Yeah, that's what we want. To be the guy in line holding up everybody else because we've got coupons.

"I'm going to be a while, lady, so stop your bitching. Besides, your milk is leaking."

There's no man that can do that. Please don't send us.

And, men, if you do get sent, there's a simple trick you can use that will help you in the future.

Screw it up.

That's what I do when it comes to shopping. I just screw it up so bad, she never sends me again.

"Honey, they were out of celery, so I got a hammer."

It'll take a while, but after you move in with a woman, everything I've talked about will become second nature. Your chores, your duties, what you can do, and more important, what you can't do.

Like bachelor parties. Can't do them anymore. Oh, she'll let me go, or at least say she doesn't care. But it's not worth all the ill will it's going to cause at home.

I'm still trying to make amends for the last one I went to. This was one of those bachelor parties where all the married men had to meet at the end of the night and go:

"OK, here's what we *say* we did."

And you make a plan.

"We got in a fight with some guys, and they ripped our underwear. That's all. That's what we say. They ripped our underwear and they smelled good. Everybody got that? Jimmy, you fell, and your nipple got pierced. It could happen! Just go with it! Come on, Jimmy, don't cave!"

There's always one guy who caves. One poor Mr. Magoo who can't hold up under his wife's cross-examination.

"We just played cards, honey . . . uh, and, and, we went to the movies, I mean, the track . . . I mean . . . OK, STRIPPERS! Dear God, they were everywhere!"

You don't see him anymore.

I know women don't really understand the concept of the bachelor party. On its face it may not make sense. Just before a man declares his eternal love and devotion to one woman for the rest of his life, he goes out for one night and packs in every decadent, raunchy activity that he can.

But you have to understand. It's like carbo loading before a marathon. Guys bulk up on strippers and alcohol so they have enough fuel to go the distance in their marriage.

Having just reread that last sentence, I'd like to issue a warning against actually using it as an explanation to your new bride.

"The guys took me out to ChestPeepers last night so I could love you forever."

Be careful, men. Women get jealous.

Most probably you won't catch any heat for your bachelor party escapades. But know this: that was your last *Get Out of Jealousy Free* card.

Women are kind of like volcanoes when it comes to jealousy. Don't be lured into complacency just because they're temporarily dormant. Always be aware that at any moment you might be running away from lava.

I'm not saying that men don't get jealous. We do. Probably more often. But women take it to a complete other level.

I never thought this until I got married. Then one day my wife came home from work mad at me because there was a pretty woman on her bus she thought I would like, had I been on the bus with her.

Let's all get this straight. I wasn't on the bus. I didn't see the woman. My wife was getting mad about how I would have reacted if I *had* seen her.

Come on, is that fair? How do you defend against that?

"But, honey, I didn't even see her."

"You would have loved her, you bastard."

And it never works the other way. She never comes home in a good mood because she walked by a florist and imagined me buying her roses.

The ways she gets mad at me never cease to amaze me. Sometimes in the morning she'll yell at me for something I've done in her *dream*.

Go ahead, laugh because it's funny. Then cry because it's true.

A dream! That's when you know you're a true married couple: when you have to apologize for what you did in her *dream*.

"Honey, I'm sorry I went skydiving and used your sister's breasts as parachutes."

Getting mad at me for things I've only done in her

mind. It just proves that when it comes to arguments, women have tools in their arsenal that completely dwarf those of men. It's like fighting an army that has nuclear bombs while your secret weapon is a sharp stick.

I will admit that I could probably make things easier on myself if I was a little more outgoing with my affection. One area I'm very negligent in is giving compliments. And, men, listen up: women like compliments.

Oh, ladies, I know I sound like an ignorant caveman. But trust me, men need to be told this.

I know I did. As I've already said, I'm not the most demonstrative man. And that can really bite you in the ass when you're married.

Whenever my wife and I argue about this subject, she still brings up the fact that I never told her how good she looked on our wedding day. That's eleven years ago. Apparently there's no statute of limitations on a violation such as that.

Of course, my argument in my defense—and this usually gets me in more trouble—is "Look, honey, we were getting married. On the day that I am dedicating myself to you for the rest of my life, can't you *assume* that I find you attractive?"

Again, laugh because it's funny, cry because she punched me.

Please, ladies, I'm not a bad person. Men just have a tough time in this area.

When we first got married, it was hard enough for me to start calling her my wife. It took me a while to make that transition.

"Guys, I'd like you to meet my girl . . . wife. My girlwife."

Engaged men, start saying "wife" now! Practice it, it's tricky!

And of course, "I love you" has always been hard for men.

"I *love* my *wife*" is practically impossible.

My wife can always tell when I've had a cocktail, because that's usually the only time I say it. It seems like it's always easier after a drink or two.

As a matter of fact, I think cops could give the drunk-driving test this way.

"Son, step out of the car and walk this line."

"Sure."

"Now touch your nose."

"No problem."

"How's your marriage?"

"I love my wife."

"You're under arrest."

.   .   .

As much as I'm advocating affection and attention toward women, sometimes you have to cut us a little slack, sisterhood.

I mean, there are times when you have to be reasonable.

When my wife and I go to bed, she tends to fall asleep right away. She's tired. I'm tired too, but I like to stay up and read a little.

That bugs her.

She'll wake up, roll over . . .

"What are you doing?"

"I'm reading."

"I thought we were going to talk to each other."

"You fell asleep."

"So right away you gotta pick up a book?"

I don't even know where to begin with that one.

She gets mad that I'm not focusing on her, even while she's *sleeping.* I guess my wife's vision of how life should be is that I pay attention to her at every waking moment, and when she falls asleep I sketch her.

I do know it's important to keep the romantic spark alive in your marriage. But with four kids, sometimes it's enough just to keep *yourself* alive.

When we first got married, our anniversary was a special day for both of us, and we'd celebrate differently each year. Now, as the years go by, the celebration has gotten less and less.

Last anniversary it was pretty much just a card. That's it. She gave me a card, I gave her one. I didn't even sign mine. I figured she knew it was from me because I was handing it to her.

"Here, honey. Whatever it says in this . . . ditto for me."

I know it sounds horrible, but we have four kids! We're tired! Things change!

Next year I'm just going to give her the $2.50.

"Honey, there was a beautiful card in that store. As a matter of fact, why don't you go there, read it, put it back, and buy us some licorice."

Throughout this chapter on marriage, you might be interpreting me as someone who has a negative attitude toward the institution. Let me just say, you are wrong.

The truth is, I thank God every day for inventing marriage. The way I see it, I'm lucky to have found a woman who will put up with me, and marriage makes it so she can't leave without a hassle.

I do make jokes about it, but I enjoy all the benefits of marriage. Intimacy, for instance. Now, I don't just mean sex. I mean the comfort factor. The beauty of really knowing somebody and, especially, having somebody really know you.

I don't want to mislead you. What I'm saying isn't as deep as it sounds. Let me try and get more specific.

It has to do with walking around naked.

It has to do with coming out of the shower and not caring about room temperature.

It has to do with not worrying anymore about the pointing and the laughing.

For the sake of the single men, let me spell it out. One of the benefits of being married is that the woman you're with already knows the potential of your penis.

I'm going to let that sit for a while.

You all right?

Probably, but let's give it another minute.*

All right. Everything's probably calmed down a little by now. Let me crack my knuckles and we'll get back into it.

What I mean by the "potential" statement is that the married man feels comfortable enough to show his

---

* Hey, Sonny Jim! Yeah, you—the eleven-year-old kid reading this in the bookstore! Close up the book and put it down, right now.

body to his wife in all phases of its, shall we say, metamorphosis.

And that's the true test of any relationship.

Some of you single guys might be saying, "Hey, my girlfriend sees me naked."

OK, but unless you've been together for a long time, when you're naked around a woman, she probably sees you only when you're at your most "impressive."

I don't think you'd be strutting right out of a cold shower in front of her, would you?

And when I say strutting, I mean with no towel. No bottle of shampoo placed strategically in front. No, shall we say, *morning stretch*. Just me and you and a dog named Boo.

You're not doing that when you're single. Especially in the beginning. No, no. And that's the difference. The married man has all but eliminated that worry from his life, simply because his wife knows all about him: the good, the bad, and the tiny.

As a matter of fact, you almost wish she was with you whenever you walked out of a shower, just so she could vouch for you.

I think any man who belongs to a gym knows what I'm talking about.

You don't want men looking at you when you're coming out of the gym shower. But you can't help thinking, "What if they do?" It's times like that, you almost want to look down at your crotch and say, "Please don't embarrass me."

Look, you just don't want them seeing you at your *least* potential. You feel like you're being misrepresented. It's like you're in court and your lawyer's blowing the case. You want to stand up and shout, "Your Honor, can I speak for myself?"

The frustrating thing is, you just have to accept it. There's nothing you can do. Because if you think the guys in the gym are looking at you funny now, try walking out of that shower at your *full* potential.

Now you've got a whole other set of problems.

In conclusion.

It's been quite a ride, this chapter, don't you think?

Let me say this about it.

After I wrote it, of course I went back and read it a few times. And while I hope it enlightens you, the reader, I found that it did something I wasn't expecting. It enlightened me.

Seeing all my inner thoughts about my marriage right there in print has made me realize a few things, none more important than this:

I love my wife.

"You've been drinking."

CHAPTER 6

Sports Guy

I don't know if there are any grooms-to-be out there who are sports fans, but if you think that after you're married you're going to watch the same amount of sports as before, just stop reading right now.

You heard me. Close the book.

You think you're gonna get married and still watch all your sports? What do you think, you have superpowers? You're probably reading this naked, because you think you're invisible. Weirdo.*

Oh, I was the same way as you. I didn't think anything would change after marriage. But I had an excuse. I was deluded because I grew up watching my mentor in this category: my father.

When my father was watching sports, it was futile

---

* This is addressed to men only. If any women reading this think they're invisible, and choose to express that belief through nudity, I'm not here to judge. But I am here. Find me.

to even attempt talking to him. If my mother had to tell him something during a game, she had a better chance going to the stadium and hanging a banner in front of the TV cameras:

**YOUR DINNER'S READY!
PULL UP YOUR PANTS AND
GET IN HERE!**

Yes, my father was a man who, as head of the family, held strong to the conviction that shutting out your loved ones to watch sports was not only a necessity but a man's right. Surely my wife would understand that that's the way I was brought up. You can't deny me my heritage.

Heritage denied.

Now, understand, I wasn't expecting the full Albert Romano sports-watching package. I understood marriage was a compromise, and I was willing to watch sports a little less, assuming things would be negotiated to our mutual satisfaction.

Here's how the final agreement worked out:

"Shut off the game, we're going to the mall."

The case is now under appeal.

If you need a little more explanation about what to expect, let me break it down for you in numbers.

Let's say that as a sports fan, on a scale of one to ten, you're an eight. You don't watch it all, but you watch a lot.

Your wife is a one. She really doesn't watch, but if she's changing channels and the guy playing the Wimbledon finals has nice legs, she might watch until the commercial. She's a *soft* one.

Your thinking goes like this: you'll probably drop down to a seven. OK, you'll watch a little less, but maybe you won't even have to, because you'll convince her that it'll be more fun if you watch together. You figure she might even come up a few points.

Son, you're leaving cookies, but Santa ain't hungry.*

What happens is, not only does she not go up, she *drops*. She hits zero and keeps going. She's in negative numbers, because now she *hates* sports. It only takes away from time you could be spending together. Sports is the enemy.

And when you factor her score in, yours can't help but get dragged down also. It's like the weather. You're an eight, but with the "wife-chill factor," it feels like a three.

Now, maybe you think, all right, I'm not watching as much sports. But when it comes to something she likes that I don't, like shopping, she's got to drop way down too.

* Meaningless phrase.

Son, when God was givin' out brains, you must have been too busy looking at your new ass.*

Write this down. When it comes to shopping, if she's an eight, she *stays* an eight, and you get dragged kicking and screaming from a one up to a six. The sad part is that it actually works out mathematically. What you go down in sports, you go up in shopping.

Say hello to everyone at the Pottery Barn!

My sports viewing now takes place mostly in the TV section of department stores.

It's sad. And we're all there, all the married men. Just shuffling around the TVs in a zombie-like stupor.

"Hi, Bill."

"Hi, Joe."

"Who's the new guy?"

"I don't know, but what's he doing up front?"

"Get in the back, pal! You're on lookout."

Thanksgiving has to be the hardest holiday to get through for a sports fan. Football is on all day and the men want to watch, but the women want to have a nice family Thanksgiving meal and share each other's company.

---

* Meaningless phrase with bad word to give it kick.

Damn them.

Last year we reached a compromise: we'd keep the TV on during dinner, but without the volume.

That's not as easy as it sounds. Now you have to pretend like you're paying attention to your family. It's hard to have a conversation when it's fourth and goal.

"Wow, everything tastes great today, Grandma. Listen, could you pass the gravy? Pass it. Pass it . . . PASS IT . . . he's *open*! Will you get rid of the GRAVY! Ohhhh . . . we shoulda got rid of her last year."

I remember during the baseball play-offs, I had invited my friend over to watch one of the games with me. Unfortunately, when he came over, he brought his fiancée with him. He didn't realize it at the time, but he'd screwed it up for both of us.

When my wife saw his fiancée, she put down what she was doing, came in the room, and wanted to start socializing. Now it would be rude to turn on the game.

What the hell was my friend thinking? What was he, a double agent?

So there we sat. Our only hope was if the women started talking to each other, we could maybe sneak off to another television, like the one I have hidden in my basement in case women ever rule the earth.

But our plan depended on the women starting to

converse, and since they didn't know each other that well, it wasn't happening.

I discovered something that day that can be very valuable to you sports fans. You can actually jump-start a conversation between two women. You just have to get the ball rolling. I did it with this phrase:

"So, Kathy, what color are your bridesmaids' dresses?"

"Oh, they're blue."

I glanced toward my wife to see if it had landed.

"Blue?"

We were almost there.

"Yes, blue. Originally I was thinking lavender, but . . ."

Boom! Game time!

If you attempt this, and right off the bat it works, just remember: don't get complacent. Every once in a while check up on them. And if you see that conversation dying down . . .

"Well, I'm sure you'll have a lovely wedding."

You have to fan those flames a little!

"Uh . . . Kathy, what about the favors?"

"Oh, little picture frames . . ."

"Really? You know I was just at a wedding where . . ."

Ba-ba-BOOM! Hello, second half!

CHAPTER 7

The Baby

After a couple gets married, it's not long until they're asking themselves:

"Are we ready for children?"

"Should we wait a couple of years?"

"When is the right time?"

You'd think the answer would be different for every couple, but having gone through it myself, I now know there's only one universal prerequisite that determines whether you're ready.

If I may, it's quite simple:

When you wake up one day and say, "You know what? I don't think I ever need to sleep or have sex again."

Congratulations, you're ready.

Now, I'm not trying to scare anybody. Everyone should have kids. They are the greatest joy in the world.

But they are also terrorists.

You'll realize this as soon as they're born and they start using sleep deprivation to break you.

Make no mistake, you are their hostage. You're going to find yourself complying with their every demand, no matter how extreme. They want you to get up and feed them at three-thirty in the morning? You don't ask questions. You say, "Is that enough milk, *sir*!"

Next time you're at the park, do yourself a favor and look at the new parents. At first glance they appear to be basking in their newfound parental bliss. But look close.

See that little facial twitch? That's no twitch, my friend. That man's a hostage and he's trying to blink you a message!

"Can't last . . . every night . . . the screams . . . the poop . . . must sleep."

Yes, it's a never-ending battle in the parental trenches, especially when it comes to sleep. Your previously uninterrupted schedule will be under constant middle-of-the-night strikes and assaults that push your troops to the brink of exhaustion. It's a common war story that parents tell all the time.

We call it "Saving Private Cryin'."

It begins with a noise. Whereas before you had kids,

the most disturbing noise you could hear during the night might have been a smoke detector or a burglar alarm, now those noises hardly compare to the horror of one barely audible:

"Wah."

It's very subtle. It's almost cute. And then it happens again.

"Wah."

At first you're in denial.

"Coulda been the radiator, honey. Or a car horn."

Then it picks up steam.

"WAHHH!"

"Honey, shut the door and turn the air conditioner on. I'm hot."

"WAHHHHHHHHHH!"

Now you panic.

"Where's my Walkman! I can't sleep without my Walkman!"

"WAHHHHHHHHHHHHHHHH!"

And then you turn on each other.

"You go!"

"No, you go!"

"IT'S YOUR *TURN*!"

In the beginning the baby has only two stages: sleeping or eating. There is a third stage—pooping—but that's more of a variable, since pooping can happen while baby is in either of the first two stages.

Perhaps it's easier to explain with math:

$$\frac{\textbf{sleep}}{\textbf{poop}} + \frac{\textbf{eat}}{\textbf{poop}} = \frac{\textbf{(sleep)} + \textbf{(eat)}}{\textbf{poop}}$$

As you can see, poop is the common denominator.

Now, the important thing to remember is that all three of these stages are independent of night and day. They happen whenever, and wherever, the baby feels necessary.

It isn't long, though, until sleep starts to adhere to a more humanlike schedule. The baby will actually start to sleep during the night and stay up during the day.*

Although this is a welcome stage, the day is harder now that baby is awake for all of it. But fear not. The long day is interrupted by one glorious element: the nap.

Ah, the nap.

Each day God bestows upon the parent one of his greatest gifts. And not a moment too soon, since you've probably spent all morning using his name in vain.

Good old God. Shrewd, ain't he?

---

* Again, this does not concern the poop. An important rule to remember during baby's first year is that poop serves no master.

But while the nap is a blessing, know this as well: it is sometimes your enemy, grasshopper.

If it sounds like I'm not making sense, then you're starting to get it. Just clear your mind and listen.

The nap can take place in three zones you should know about: Normal, Hot, and Point of No Return.

Here's how it works.

Let's say a baby normally goes to sleep for the night at seven. Now, each baby is different, but this baby, whom we will call Hypothetical, also takes a nap from noon until two.

You got it?

Naptime is from twelve till two, bedtime is at seven.

OK, so let's say you're at the park with little Hypo. He's having fun, you're not looking at the time, and the next thing you know, it's 12:30.

Right now you're still safe. You're in the Normal Zone, which is roughly an hour on either side of his usual nap starting time. He can take his nap anytime in that zone, and there'll be no major ramifications.

But let's say you push it.

And you always push it, don't ya?

Hypo made a friend in the sandbox, and now it's 1:15.

Nice going, Sexy. You just entered the Hot Zone.

It's not a disaster yet, but now you have to hurry. In the Hot Zone he's passed his naptime, but if you get him to sleep *right now,* you can prevent any major sleep-schedule catastrophe.

OK. Here we go.

Let's say that you realize you're in the Hot Zone. So now you have to get Hypo back home, pronto. You pick him up, wipe the sand off his ass, strap him in the car, and you're on your way. You'll take the parkway because it's a little quicker than the side streets.

Bad move. There's a jackknifed chicken truck in the center lane, and traffic's at a crawl. In twenty minutes you move a hundred yards. That ain't gonna cut it.

Welcome to zone three. The Point of No Return.

Your world just turned topsy-turvy, because now, instead of trying to get him to sleep, you have to keep him *awake.* Suddenly what's good is bad, what's up is down, what's fat is skinny.

Let me explain.

At this point it's so far past his naptime, you have to try to keep him awake until bedtime. Because if he naps now . . .

Well, let me use my old pal math:

$$\text{naptime} \leq 1{:}00 \ = \ \text{bedtime} \leq 7{:}00$$
$$\text{naptime} \geq 2{:}00 \ = \ \text{bedtime} \geq X$$

X of course is unknown. The only thing known about X is that somewhere in it, instead of watching

ER, you're going to be in your boxer shorts putting on a puppet show.

So in the Point of No Return Zone, you've got to accept that naptime can't happen, and redirect your energy toward keeping Hypo awake at all costs. But in this scenario there's a catch.

YOU'RE IN THE *CAR*!

Every parent knows that for a kid, the car is chloroform.

It's your best friend when you're trying to get the kid to sleep. That's what works with my kids. As a matter of fact, that's our nighttime ritual: brush the teeth, read a story, Long Island Expressway.

But now the tide has turned. You gotta get him out of that car, because you don't want him to sleep and you can't risk driving another minute.

Anytime you put a kid in the car, you just don't know how far you can travel until he's out.

What parents need—and I wish someone would look into this—is a "nap pressure gauge." Come on, NASA. Just come up with something simple, some kind of valve that every service station would have, so you could just pull over, pop it in your kid's ear, and see how much consciousness is left in him.

"Sir, your son's got eight more driving minutes left. Now, we can give him a Pepsi, but that's only gonna buy you five more. Your best bet is to leave him overnight, and while he's here we'll put him up on the lift and check out that smell."

Of course, once your kid gets older and can talk, you have a fighting chance of trying to keep him awake because you have access to a new tactic: lies.

"I see Godzilla!"

"Where, Dad?"

"Keep looking!"

It's when they can't talk that you have a real challenge. You open windows, turn on the radio, sing the Barney song.

Everyone has their own method. I'm not proud of mine, but I'll pass it on.

Water gun.

One thing you will find out is how quickly you learn the tricks of the parenting trade.

And by that I don't mean anything you may have read in a book or that you know to be traditional child-rearing common sense. I mean the fly-by-the-seat-of-your-pants way you handle situations. If you have a second kid, you'll laugh at some of the things you did when you were a freshman parent.

You can always tell the freshmen. They're the ones

who find their baby's pacifier on the floor and get on the phone to the Poison Control Center.

When you get to four children, like us, if you find a pacifier under the couch, you blow off the dust bunny and pop it back into circulation.

Freshmen never let the child out of their sight. Whereas, with four kids, you're happy if you know where three of them are.

Don't get me wrong. Just because you have more kids doesn't mean you stop being a good parent. You just know the ins and outs. You know the shorthand. You're a pro. But believe me, the magic of parenthood never wears off. As a matter of fact, since we've just become parents again for the fourth time, I'm enjoying all those newborn things I forgot about.

Their goofy look. Their smile. That baby scent. Not to mention what I think is the coolest:

You can take their pulse just by looking at their head.

The pulsating soft spot. Man, those are cool. I wish those stayed with you. I'd love to have one just so I could look in the mirror and know when to get off the treadmill.

"Wow, maximum heart rate already!"

You should always check the soft spot after your

baby is born. Just make sure it's there, and make sure that it curves *in*.

If it doesn't . . . if it's popped *out,* that means he's been tampered with. Somebody tried to unscrew his head. That's my theory.

I like a big head on a baby. Which is why my six-month-old baby's head really excites me. It's about two feet across.

Joseph is one giant guy. You can already tell he's going to be some kind of athlete. I hope I'm not sounding like one of those parents who always brag about their kids. I've dealt with those guys.

A friend of mine had a baby just about the same time we had Joe, and he's constantly updating me as to all his accomplishments.

"Rolled over already. Only three months old, and he rolled over."

"Yeah, that's good."

"Hear what I said? He *rolled over*. They don't usually do that until four months."

"I heard you."

I don't want to be that kind of parent, but sometimes you find that it's hard not to get sucked into the game.

"How's Joe? He's four months, right? Did he roll over yet?"

"Yes. Yes, he did. The other day I was watching him. He was lying on his back, and he rolled over onto his belly."

"Well, like I said, at four months that's normal."

"Right. Then, while he was on his belly . . . push-ups. He started doing push-ups."

"What?"

"Yeah, push-ups. The ones where you clap in the middle."

One thing I know I can safely brag about with baby Joe is his consistency in waking up every morning surrounded by a smell he didn't go to bed with.

What's amazing is how I let it catch me off guard every time. I wake up, and there he is with that little bubbly face. I dive right in for that morning smooch, and WHAMMO! It's like he just pulled the pin on an odor grenade.

Every morning. You'd think I would catch on, but I can't help myself. He makes all these cute noises, he's got that little smile.

Sometimes I think he knows what he's doing. Like it's almost a game for him.

"I'll make with a little goo-goo here . . . that should suck him in. Come on, Daddy. Don't I look cute in these feety pajamas? Let's go . . . you haven't seen me in eight hours. You know you want to snuggle. Come on. Here he comes . . . a little closer, little closer . . . ahhhhhhhhhh, *skunked* ya! Hoo-hoo, look at him run."

We have a saying in our house that kind of sums up the whole experience:

"You can't start the morning without a hot cuppa Joe."

I know it's a pun, but you gotta give me that one.

After I give him that morning kiss, the next step is to make sure he gets changed. So I step back a few feet, get myself together, take a deep breath, and go wake up my wife.

I'm kidding, of course. I would never shirk my responsibility. And besides, how could I ever pass up a visit to the magical world of diapers?

Oh, what an enchanted land that is. For those of you who've never been, you're in for a treat.

When you open a newborn's diaper for the first time, it's like watching fireworks. A rainbow of colors, a lot of ooohs and aahs, and if you're not careful, you lose a finger.

The changing of a diaper is always a process that takes some getting used to. When starting out, there are many things you should be prepared for. There is a lot of advice I could burden you with, but none more important than to always keep alert.

Especially with boys.

We had a girl first. And when your first venture into

diaper land is with a baby girl, you get a very false sense of security. Aside from aromatically, you're never in any real danger. I don't know if you need me to spell it out, but I will:

With a girl, nothing is pointed at you.

With a boy, as soon as that diaper opens up, there's an infrared light on your forehead.

And you never see it coming. You're still on a new-parent high.

"Aw, look how cute—"

SQUIRT!

"Mornin', Poppa!"

You can't lollygag with a boy. You gotta be *quick*. Just get in and get out!

Sometimes you try double-teaming him. You wipe while your wife powders. Everything's moving along smoothly until you get tangled in the Velcro flap, and you can sense he's locking in on you. Your wife starts screaming.

"Don't be a hero! Get *out*!"

SQUIRT!

"Keep the change."

The best thing to do is accept that you're going to get hit sooner or later, because they're that good. They're sharpshooters.

We had twin boys, which was even worse because they compete with each other.

"You didn't think I could reach him from here, did you?"

"That's nothing. Watch this, I'll put his cigarette out."

As your child gets older, the diaper stage takes on a whole different dynamic.

If you've ever seen a kid poop in his diaper *standing up*, you know what I'm talking about. If you ask me, it's why man invented the video camera.

It's quite a funny sight. And you can always tell when it's happening.

When everything's normal, they're running around the room at a hundred miles an hour. It's when you catch that sudden slowdown in the action that you know it's time to plug in the Handycam.

Suddenly, instead of running, they're walking. Then they're pacing, and finally they come to a complete stop. Just standing in one spot. Although in some instances you might be able to detect a slight rocking.

Then they get an odd look on their face. It's sort of a slight grimace with a "why me" in their eyes. The back arches a little. And then the dead giveaway, the shuffle behind the furniture.

If you see your diaper-clad child with that face on, wedged into a little nook and cranny somewhere behind the couch, it's *go time*.

In some cases you might witness what I call "the Leaner." It's everything mentioned above, with a little extra strain in his face as he bends over slightly at the waist, putting one hand on the couch arm for support.

Never make eye contact with "the Leaner." He's like a pit bull, and if he sees you looking at him, you're going to get a face full of growl.

"ARRRRRRRRRRGH! ARRRRRRRRRRRRRR-RRRRRRRRRRRRRRRRR!"

Oddly enough, as an adult, things really don't change that much. Sure, you probably don't have people watching you, but there's always some idiot knocking on the bathroom door. You still growl, only now it's:

"I'M IN HERE!"

OK, we've talked about sleeping and napping and diapers. But we can't wrap up the chapter on the baby without filling you in on one other major adjustment you will have to make in your life.

Are you sitting down? Because this is the sex talk.

Once again I'm going to express this mathematically.

The amount of sex you have after the baby is equal to the amount of sex you had before the baby minus the amount of sex you had before the baby.

Or:

sex before baby
− sex before baby

= sex after baby

Of course, there is a plus- or minus-one margin of error.

How can it be minus one, you ask? How can you have negative sex? Well, Slick, when you have a baby, your level of tiredness can get so high that you begin to lose even the *memory* of sex.

And it's not a one-sided drop-off, it's mutual. She's tired. You're tired. The baby's crying. You're crying.

Even when the baby falls asleep, you have to choose.

"Should we have sex or go to sleep?"

"Look, I'm going to sleep. You can do whatever you want."

And remember, that's only after *one* child. We have four. Sex for my wife and me is . . . well . . . she won't be happy I'm mentioning it, but here it is:

Every three months.

That's right, I said it, and I'm glad I did. I don't care if I get in trouble, I have to tell somebody. There's no support group for me out there.

It's every three months. We don't plan it that way, that's just how it turns out.

You know what I do? Every time we have sex, the next day I pay my estimated tax.

It's the truth. If we have sex, my quarterlies are due. There. Now you know it all.

If it's oral sex, I renew my driver's license.

CHAPTER 8

The Two-Year-Old

My first encounter with a two-year-old came after I had gotten married and become an uncle to my wife's nephew.

Until that day I wasn't really that informed about the two-year-old. Oh, I'd read about them, and occasionally I'd see documentaries on the Discovery Channel showing two-year-olds in the wild, where they belong.

But my new nephew was the first one I had seen up close. And let me tell you: if you're ever out on a safari and come across one like this, stay in the Jeep.

My wife hates when I start talking about him like this.

"He's your nephew. You should love him."

I'm not saying I don't love him. I just don't want him *in my house*.

Why can't I love him from afar? That's how I want to love him—through pictures and folklore.

I suppose everyone knows a monster two-year-old, but nobody tops my nephew. I'm telling you, if I could have gotten a restraining order against him, I would have. I don't know what legal action you can take against a two-year-old, but I think I had a case. I could have just shown the judge everything he'd broken in my house.

"Please, Your Honor, look around. Look at what he's done! Look at my cat, *Hop-a-long*. That was *Flash*! His name used to be *Flash*. Is that enough evidence, or should I call my dog, *Cyclops*, to the stand?"

My nephew's whole mission in life was to come into our house and break stuff as quickly as he could. Each time he'd try to beat his own record.

"Vase! Ashtray! Statue! Gimme the time."

"Twenty-eight seconds."

"Set 'em up again."

It got to the point where I would just follow him around with a calculator and give his mother the bill when they left. Sometimes they'd walk in, and she'd just hand me a fifty.

"Look, cut him off when he gets to this."

During my firstborn's two-year-old phase, something very unique happened. All of a sudden I found I was offering myself up to do a lot of chores. Not all chores. No, no, there was a certain trend to my domestic philanthropy: getting out of the house.

"Anybody need anything, from . . . the Motor Vehicle Bureau? Can I register anything for anyone? It's no problem. I'll go. I was going out anyway to apply for jury duty."

It wasn't until I had a two-year-old that I would actually look forward to a dentist appointment. To most people the dentist just means pain. To me? *Sitting.* Not only that, but for once *I* get to do the drooling.

Things other people found annoying, I now appreciated.

Traffic.

Ah, sweet traffic.

How could you could not like traffic? It's quiet, you're sitting, and no one's pouring paint in a fishbowl.

I spent a lot of time in my car then. Half of it was just to use the cell phone. I learned the hard way not even to attempt a business call from my house if my two-year-old was in the area.

"Yeah, the fifteenth is good for me. I just need to know where do you . . . thiNK YOU'RE GOING WITH THAT *COOKIE*!!! PUT THE COOKIE *DOWN*! Oh . . . not you. Sorry. Did I scare you? Oh . . . didn't know you were eating a cookie."

· · ·

You can't even hope to slow a two-year-old down. I don't know if you've ever tried to pick one up and carry him against his will, but know this: you can't do it.

They all have the same martial arts move. They're born with it. You try to lift them and they activate the Anti-Lift Slide.

It goes something like this. You've got your hands under his armpits, and you're carrying him. You've walked about three steps, and suddenly he flings his arms straight up in the air, which allows him, in a way that scientists don't fully understand, to double his body weight.

And then, with a quick wiggle sometimes accompanied by a defiant scream, he slides through your hands like a greased watermelon, and hits the ground running. It's so fast sometimes, you don't even notice he's gone until he's down the hall, kicking the dog.

There are times when he will actually let you pick him up. You carry him a few feet, he's made no attempt at escape, and you begin to think you've broken his spirit like you would a wild horse.

But don't get too sure of yourself. You don't even know what's going on, you poor stupid bastard. He hasn't given in. He just wants to go somewhere, and you're his ride. It feels like you're in charge, but trust me, you've got to take him exactly where he wants to go. If you try to put him down before that . . .

Say hello to "Mr. Jelly Legs."

It always catches you by surprise. There you are, trying to release him, but his legs just won't lock in. And you can't let him go because he'll hit his head on the coffee table. He knows it, and he knows you know it.

And he's just looking up at you, saying, "Oh, no. Not here, Big Person. You're the one who wanted to lift me. Well, I'm not going down until I'm within arm's reach of a cookie jar."

They're geniuses.

Over the years the two-year-old has developed many of these impressive defense mechanisms. But let's not sell the parents short. We've come up with a few strategies of our own to counteract them. None more impressive than the legendary Count of Three.

How many times have you heard a parent say, "I'm going to give you until the count of three . . ."

It's a proven technique that was developed when it became apparent that "do it right *now*" seldom got the job done.

The Count of Three works because it gives the kid the impression that he's negotiating with you. "All right, Mom, we've heard your demands, and we're willing to accept them. But here's what we want: three seconds."

It's a universal, worldwide, amazing phenomenon. It even transcends language.

You could be a kid in a tribe in Papua New Guinea that doesn't even use words. Whatever it is, you're still going to get *three* of them. Go ahead, try sneaking a few bites of coconut before finishing up all your gazelle meat. You know what Mom's gonna give you? Two clicks and a clack to put that shell *down*!

It's a standard. Three.

I've seen parents who try to go outside the norm.

There was a kid I saw in a supermarket once whose mom was trying to get him to put back a candy bar. And with my own ears I heard her say to him, "I'm giving you to the count of *two*."

Two?

Right there I witnessed firsthand why three was the chosen number.

The kid had no chance with two! He couldn't have made it back to the candy aisle even if he tried! His only hope was to hand it off to some kid who had three.

"Please . . . take this the rest of the way for me. She's a psycho."

You can't give any less than three. It's not humane.

On the other hand, you can't go over three, either, because you'll lose credibility. Which poses a problem when a parent can see that the kid is gonna require a little more time.

Which brings us to the Fraction Loophole.

"Two and a half. Two and *three-quarters* . . ."

It's really a thing of beauty. You can give the kid as long as you want, and you haven't broken the sacred code of three.

My mom used to do this. But when she got to two and three-quarters, we knew we had to move fast, because she didn't know any more fractions.

As wild as a two-year-old is, take solace in knowing that they do have their quiet moments. Sometimes you get lucky. Sometimes they hit a lull. Like the hurricane's eye, the two-year-old will allow you a few moments of peace before he tears your house off its foundation and destroys your crops.

The peace is beautiful while it lasts. There he is, for one glorious moment, in the corner of the house entertaining himself with something very quiet and small and nonbreakable.

That's what we lose as adults—the ability to be easily entertained. Think of what it takes to keep you occupied now. You've got to go to movies, out for drinks, dancing.

If a two-year-old is bored, you know what can hold him over for ten minutes?

Arm swinging.

Just standing with both feet planted, twisting his torso and swinging his arms around. Clockwise, counterclockwise, clockwise, counterclockwise. Faster, slower. It's like his own little party.

When he gets tired of that, he might move on to a noise. Just a noise. He'll discover a new noise he can make and go with it.

"Ladel ladel *ladel ladel* LADEL LADEL ladel ladel . . ."

High, low, soft, loud. Sometimes he combines them. He'll go wild. He'll arm swing *and* ladel. Don't bother him now because the carnival's in town.

Wouldn't that be great as an adult if that's all you needed? You'd never have a bad time.

"Hey, Bill, you should have seen this bachelor party. The stripper never showed, but we all started *ladeling* . . ."

Of course, while it's great to see your two-year-old child entertaining himself quietly, you have to stay aware of the fact that it's only going to last ten minutes.

And that's the downside. To a two-year-old, everything is interesting for a maximum of ten minutes. It could be arm-swinging, it could be a puppy. It could be arm-swinging a puppy. It's still only going to be ten minutes, and then he's on to something else.

Which is why when you shop for a toy for a two-year-old, there's only one criterion: cheap. It's not because *you* are cheap, it's because you know that whatever it is you bring home its entertainment value won't last long.

Before you know it, it gets retired to the bottom of the toy box. Sometimes it'll make a comeback, but probably not in a way you'll be happy about. You'll know what I mean when you see your daughter using her old Cabbage Patch Doll as a paintbrush.

You can always tell nonparents by the type of gift they buy for your kids.

We had a single friend we invited over for dinner who took it upon himself to surprise our kids with a present. It was a bright green gooey toy called Gak.

I wish I was still punching him.

I'm going to make it easy for the nonparents. Here's a quick list of what to never buy for your friend's two-year-old:

1) **Anything that has the word "silly" in it.**
Parents know that "silly" is a code word meaning "doesn't come out of the carpet."
2) **Anything that has "rapid reload."**
3) **Anything that says "Some Assembly Required."**

That's the biggest understatement in the history of advertising. My daughter's tricycle said "Some Assembly Required."

It came in a jar.

4) **Anything that involves the hose.**

5) **Anything that has a name that isn't really a word.**

For example, Gak.

6) **Anything that says "Adult Supervision Required."**

Don't bring over a gift like this unless *you're* planning to be the adult.

And finally,

7) **Anything that makes a noise that, repeated a hundred times, would make you cry.**

Of course there are some products that I hope you'd know to avoid just by the name:

"Lil' Wall Painter"

"Airborne Ink"

"Baby's First Staple Gun"

To name a few.

Look, the perfect gift is anything that keeps their attention for a while and doesn't require a mop.

You know what your best bet is? Just tell them a story. Kids like stories. They're fun, they're not messy, everybody wins.

But here's a little bit of advice. If you think you're going to entertain your friends' kids with a funny story or a joke, it better have the word "poop," "fart," or "heinie" in it, or you're going down in flames.

Don't try to be cerebral. You're not going to win them over with political humor unless the joke is about how "Congress has just passed a law outlawing poop."

Recently my friend and I had an argument because he tried to tell me that looking after his dog, Pepper, was just as difficult as taking care of my then two-year-old daughter, Alexandra.

I wish I was still punching him.

We argued back and forth. To me the argument was ludicrous. I wasn't even going to waste my time, but then he got all in my face with:

"What? You clean up poop, I clean up poop. Your kid throws up, my dog throws up. Your kid cries, my dog barks. It's all the same."

For a minute I actually thought he had a point. Then my two-year-old hit me in the head with an ashtray, and I was brought back to my senses.

Look, this dog-versus-kid argument takes place all

the time, and parents usually lose because they're too exhausted to defend themselves. So I've taken it upon myself to make things a little easier for all of you out there.

The next time a friend of yours says something stupid like "I know what being a parent is like—I've got a poodle," don't waste your breath.

Just reach into your pocket and whip out this chart, courtesy of yours truly:

BAD THING	DOG	TWO-YEAR-OLD
Climbs into your bed	✓	✓
Pees in it		✓
Has dirty diapers		✓
Repeats curse words		✓
Must be strapped in a car seat		✓
Sees toys on TV, cries until you buy them		✓
Sticks keys into outlets		✓
Falls down stairs		✓
Gets charged full fare on an airline		✓
Requires paid sitter while you go to a movie		✓
Wears sneakers		✓
Needs to watch Barney		✓
Throws food on floor		✓
Attracts attention if left tied to the fire hydrant outside a supermarket		✓
Grows up and writes a book about you		✓
Has bad breath	✓	

.   .   .

You're welcome.

Parents, be confident. In all the world, there's only one thing that compares to a two-year-old:

Another two-year-old.

(See next chapter.)

CHAPTER 9

The Twins

OK, I think I established in that last chapter just how much destruction a two-year-old is capable of.

Now, close your eyes and do me a favor.

Picture two of them.

Anything coming up? It's not registering, right? You just can't conceive of such carnage.

Well, that image that is beyond the capability of the human brain to imagine is my *reality*. Look, I can't blame you for drawing a blank. I lived through it, and *I* don't know how to describe it. There's really only one example I can give.

Did you see the movie *Twister*?

It's very similar. You might think that's an exaggeration but believe me, if you leave twin two-year-olds alone in your living room, at some point a cow will be airborne.

Each one alone is only capable of a certain limited amount of damage. It's when they're together that they find out their true potential. They don't just double the damage when they're together, oh no, it's much more than that, because now they're *inspired*.

It's scary. The last thing one two-year-old needs is another one right behind him *cheering him on*.

"Throw it. You can throw that! That's right, now *jump*! You can jump from there! Don't be afraid . . . I did that jump when I was *one*. Come on, get down here and make it fast. We gotta stick things in the toilet! For God's sake, we're already behind schedule, and today's Ink Day! Aww, you're gonna love the things I got planned for ink. Now let's go, and if you see Mom and Dad, just play up that cute crap."

They're quite a team. What one does the other does. There's no real chain of command. Each one of them takes turns leading the charge. They're identical twins in every sense of the word.

Of course, you could see very early that like most boys, they were going to be competitive.

I don't know when sibling rivalry usually starts, but at my wife's first sonogram it looked like the fetus on top had the other one in a headlock. For nine months, the guy on the bottom was getting pounced on. I felt bad for him until he finally figured out a way to retaliate: pinching the other guy's umbilical cord.

"How's that feel, Headlock Brother? You're the big

tough man up there, right? What's the matter—getting a little hungry?"

They were both six pounds, seven ounces when they were born, which is a pretty good total amount of baby. They were an hour and a half apart, which is a little peculiar for twins, but how can you blame the second guy for taking his time? It was the first time he had the place to himself.

"Now this is more like it! Let's just hope Ugly doesn't find his way back."

Of course, the advantage to being the first one out of the womb is that you are, and always will be, the older brother. Yes, it's usually only a matter of minutes we're talking about, but nonetheless you are older. And being older has its traditional advantages. At first it won't make a difference, but by the time they become teenagers, the younger twin will have been subject to the same problems all younger siblings have.

"Dad, why can't I have the car? You always let Gregory use it."

"Well, hold on here, young man. When you're *his* age . . . hold on . . . not yet, not yet . . . OK, *now*. Now you can have the car. Too late. Gregory took it."

No matter how you slice it, twin or no twin, if you've got a brother who is older than you, he's going to take advantage of his seniority. That's what older brothers do—try their best to make your life miserable.

Take it from this younger brother who still has the first poem he ever wrote, entitled "A Noogie Makes Me Cry."

My twins are identical.

I think if you're going to have twins, they should always be identical. That's the fun part of twins. I'm not saying fraternal twins aren't great also, I'm just saying there's certain bonuses that you get when they're identical.

First of all, without identical twins, you'll never get to experience entering a hotel room with one of them and watching him run into the full-length mirror because he thought he saw his brother.

True story.*

But the reason I like identical the most is simple: you save money on photographs.

"See that picture? That's my little boy . . . and I got another one just like him."

.   .   .

---

* Look, I want to stress that that story is true, because it sounds like I contrived it just to be cute. Homey don't play that.

The only downside I can find to identical twins is that no one besides you and your wife can tell them apart. Oh, it's fun in the beginning, because you feel like you have superpowers. When friends are over you show off.

"Go ahead. I'm not looking—mix 'em up and get your bets down."

It's really no great mystery. Every set of twins has some little tiny difference that the parents can recognize. Sometimes it's a freckle, a clump of hair, a birthmark.

With my guys? Head girth.

Not width, not depth. *Girth.* It's hard to pinpoint where one's head is girthier than the other, but there is a difference. It's actually easier for me to tell them apart from behind. Assuming they're not wearing hats.

You can't teach someone how to tell them apart. The only way to really acquire the power is through time. Which is why some relatives are better than others. The twice-a-year uncle is never going to get it.

Then again, my mother, who spends a lot of time with them, still has problems.

She's a little neurotic, and when she babysits for them she gets nervous. Her big fear is that she's going to keep feeding the same one over and over. When they were babies, my wife and I never wanted to go on vacation because we were afraid there'd be a big fat one when we came home.

"Oh, Mom, what did you do to the twins? Look at them. They're Siskel and Ebert."

It didn't help that my wife would dress them alike.

To tell them apart, my mother developed her own little system: she'd put a Band-Aid on one of their fingers.

One night while my mom was babysitting, she discovered we were out of Band-Aids. When my wife and I came home, she told us she didn't have a problem, though, because one of the twins had a little scratch on his nose.

That's what she used to tell them apart. The scratch.

That kind of scared me because, as hard as I tried, I didn't remember the scratch being there when we left the house.

I know that's a ridiculous thought, but all I could picture was my mother finding no Band-Aids, starting to panic, and rationalizing that putting a little nick on a nose wouldn't hurt anybody.

Scccccratch . . . !

"OK, let me write this down. Gregory has a scratch on his nose . . . and, he's a crybaby."

My biggest worry about having identical twins is what they will look like when they get older.

Right now they're five years old, and no matter what, they're cute. Anytime you see young identical *anything*—puppies, boys, pandas—it's automatically cute because they look alike.

When they become adults, that theory doesn't apply anymore. I know everyone hopes their children grow up to be attractive, but if you have identical twins, there's a little extra pressure.

Because with twins, even if they're *slightly* ugly as adults, that's going to be magnified.

There's two of them. People will notice that.

I mean, think about it. If you see one slightly ugly man walking across a room, that's no big deal. But if you see the same ugliness, right behind him . . . *that* you're going to notice.

"You know something? I didn't think the first guy was that ugly, until I saw it *again*."

One final bit of advice to anyone out there who may one day be the parent of twins: be very careful how you name them.

As a matter of fact, this goes out to all parents. Naming your child is extremely tricky. You have to remember that kids will torture other kids with any name joke they can possibly make.

Now, many times it's unavoidable. I'm sorry, but if you're an overweight boy named Pat, we all know what's going to happen. That's the simple rule of the rhyme. It's like the misfortune of being an aromatically challenged kid named Kelly.

But some names, you almost have to admire the ingenuity kids use to find the joke. I remember a kid in camp named Herman. Sounds like a safe name, right? You think, what could they possibly get out of Herman?

Sperm-man. OK? Sperm-man is what they can get out of Herman. Parents, just keep in mind that kids will always round off to the nearest obscenity.

Now with twins, I don't know what it is, but parents have a natural instinct to give them those soundalike, same-initial, cutesy names.

"Hey, meet our twins, Timmy and Tommy."

Once again, it's cute when they're four, but by ten they're in therapy.

Each twin needs to have his own personality, and that should start with the name. It should be unique in and of itself, and not dependent on the sibling. That's the healthiest thing you can do for them as parents.

I can see different personalities already starting to develop in my boys.

Gregory's the independent one, outgoing and daring and not afraid to try anything.

Schmegory . . . well, he's got a few problems.*

---

* His real name is Matthew and he's fine.

A NOOGIE MAKES ME CRY
By Ray Romano, age 7

Sitting in my room
Trying to watch TV
I hear a noise downstairs.
Who could that be?

I open up the door
Just trying to spy.
I hope it's not my brother
A noogie makes me cry.

The hallway light goes on
I hear footsteps on the stairs.
Who could it be?
Am I the only one who cares?

I hope it's a burglar
And I'll tell you why.
Because then it's not my brother
A noogie makes me cry.

I hide in the corner
As he opens the door.
Is it my brother?
I just peed on the floor.

Oh, look it's my mom!
And she brought me some pie!
For now I am happy
But a noogie makes me cry.

CHAPTER 10

Everything and a Kite

This here is a chapter of things my kids have said.

You heard me.

Look, all parents make you listen to stories about the things their kids have said.

These are mine.

Get back here! Look, just read them. It'll be over before you know it.

Just to let you know, there's no semblance of order to these stories, they're not related to each other, but for no particular reason I have titled them.

Once again, just things they've said.

All right, you could jump over this chapter and go right to the next, but honestly, what are you afraid of?

Nonna You Fuck

Good start, right?

Before I begin this story, I want to make the point that while my book is not completely profanity free, not one curse is used gratuitously. I'm not a comic who uses foul language for shock value, but I will use it if it serves the story.

In this particular case it *is* the story.

Inevitably, a toddler is going to hear, and then repeat, a profanity. Just accept it. Unless your son's name is Opie, at some point in toddlerhood you're going to hear a gleeful, high-pitched curse.

New parents, listen closely. Your first instinct might be to laugh, or perhaps scold.

No.

The only correct response is to *ignore*.

Absolutely, positively ignore. Don't bring any attention to it whatsoever.

And by all means, don't do what I did: videotape it. Learn from me.

The first time one of my two-year-olds repeated a curse, I'll admit, it was funny, and I laughed.

Little did I know I had created a monster.

Listen, when a two-year-old sees that he can get a reaction from Mommy and Daddy, his thought pattern is this:

"I do again."

And he did it quite often.

It never really posed much of a problem, because we were the only ones who he would say it to.

Then one day my eighty-seven-year-old grandmother was over the house.

Of course, the title of this story gives away the ending, but that's how it went down. An eighty-seven-year-old, playfully jostling a two-year-old, and then . . .

"Nonna, you f***." *

My wife and I froze, hoping it didn't register.

"Nonna, you f***."

That one was loud and clear. What followed was a "Nonna you f***" medley. All types of deliveries. Singsong, rapid-fire, couple of hold-the-last-noters, and my personal favorite, the gravelly-voice one with a scream chaser.

He just kept at it as Nonna watched and watched.

Now, as far as what happened afterward, I'm almost afraid to tell you. I don't want future parents to take the consequences of a cursing baby lightly. This story should serve as a warning to them and not as something amusing. But I'm not going to hold back the truth. Here's what happened.

---

* Look, you know what he's saying. I just don't want to desensitize you to the word, in case I need to use it later.

As the barrage of "Nonna you f***"s continued, Grandma turned to me and with a puzzled look said:

"I think he wants fudge."

We didn't deserve to be that lucky. She had no idea what he was saying. The more he said it, the hungrier she thought he was. She gave him some fudge and was never the wiser.

No one was hurt, no one was offended, and we let out a huge sigh of relief.

Of course soon after that we realized that our two-year-old had a whole new thought pattern.

Say f***, get fudge.

Gimme the Salt

OK, let's be honest. Any story that has to follow "Nonna" is gonna have its work cut out for it. But look, somebody had to step up, and it's "Gimme the Salt."

It's short and sweet and here it is.

Dinner table. Wife and kids. Middle of the meal. Matthew, then four years old, chirps:

"Gimme the salt, Daddy."

Me, trying to instill manners:

"What's the magic word?"

Matthew, with total sincerity:

"Abracadabra."

Like I said, it's no "Nonna" story.

But it happened, it's cute, now move on.

The Law

It was a heated conversation between my then five-year-old daughter, Alexandra, and her five-year-old cousin Sandy that brought back a lost memory of childhood.

They were playing together. Things were going fine. Sandy happened to have a pocketful of candy.

Now, anytime two kids are playing together and only one has candy, I get a little antsy. Nothing major. It's like I can't get comfortable in my chair, or the back of my neck itches. Kind of the way an animal will act peculiar right before an earthquake.

Anyway, Sandy had candy. Alexandra didn't.

Alexandra asked Sandy for a piece.

Sandy said no.

I ran behind the couch.

Alexandra tried again, and was again refused. It was on the third try that Alexandra made her threat.

"If you don't give me some candy, you're not my cousin anymore."

And there it was. I had forgotten one of the greatest aspects of childhood. It was pure, it was simple, and it was being enacted right before me.

The laws that govern the little.

As silly as "you're not my cousin anymore" sounds to adults, to a five-year-old, it's serious business.

At five years old, you can have your cousinhood annulled verbally!

It was a valid threat, and it worked! Sandy coughed up some candy, real quick.

You can't help but admire the simplicity of the kiddie legal system. No lawyers, no paperwork. Just words. Yet so many legal areas are covered.

Insurance. Insurance was big back then.

You're playing stickball and you've got a new ball that cost you a dollar twenty-five.

Before the game starts you make an announcement.

"Chips on the ball, everybody."

Bingo, you just bought insurance. Now, if someone loses that ball, hits it on the roof, throws it down a sewer, you're covered. That person is responsible for reimbursing you.

You called chips. That was insurance.

"Dibs," on the other hand, was how you staked your claim to something that wasn't yours yet.

Dad's driving to the hardware store. He asks if you and your brother want to come along. Without wasting a precious second, you shout:

"Dibs on the front seat!"

Now you can take your sweet time getting to the

car. You wanted a certain piece of real estate, and "dibs" was your down payment.

"Dibs" could be tricky, though. Like with any legal contract, you had to be on guard against the loopholes. At any moment, your brother could shout:

"Dibs on the front seat . . . *on the way back.*"

It was a simple system, but you had to know all the ins and outs, or you could end up in the backseat, sitting on the hump, until you had your own car.

Let's not forget "no backsies." No backsies was the verbal binding of a deal.

You want your friend's tuna sandwich and talk him into trading it for your banana. You make the exchange. As he hands it to you, you say to his face:

"No backsies."

Seconds later, he realizes the banana is bruised and he's made a horrible mistake. He wants his tuna sandwich back.

TOO LATE!

You have a binding contract: no backsies.

The boy cries.

Oh, if only we had the same system among adults. Simple, pure, and cheap.

Of course, once you become an adult, you realize the necessity of our complicated legal system. Yes, it'd be nice to get rid of all the red tape, but think of how high the divorce rate would be if all it took was:

"You're not my wife anymore."

———

Then again, you might think twice if all she had to say was:

"Dibs on all your money."

Judy and Nancy and Karen and Susan and Mary

One of the privileges kids have is that no matter what they say, it can be construed as cute. It doesn't have to make sense, it doesn't have to be rational, it's just cute.

One day my daughter came into our room and told us that she had named her toes. She had a name for every toe.

"This is Judy and Nancy and Karen and Susan and Mary."

When I tell people that story they think it's adorable.

Which is fine. But how come if Grandpa does it, it's a tragedy?

Nobody's ooh-ing and ah-ing then. Last thing you want during dinner is Grandpa sticking his foot up on the table.

"Say hello to Fat Tony and Jimmy the Weasel."

Bathtub Fun

Many childhood escapades take place in the bathtub. I'm not sure why that is, but I think it has to do with the combination of kids, water, and naked.

It was during bathtime for my then two-year-old twins that one of them stood up so he could show me something. I don't know how to tactfully describe what it was, except to say, I guess the water had *stimulated* him.

Are you getting the image? I hope so. And let me let you in on something. Two-year-olds have very little inhibition when it comes to their bodies. On the contrary, they're proud. What they have, they want to announce to everyone. And so he did.

"Pee-pee big! Pee-pee big! Pee-pee BIG!"

Catchy, isn't it?

"Pee-pee BIG."

On and on he went, hands at his sides and grin on his face.

I had to admit, he was cute.

Of course, once again: Grandpa does it, not so cute.

Everything and a Kite

It happened last January. I was sitting at the kitchen table with one of my twins. He was eating a bowl of Cap'n Crunch and I was buttering my toast. We weren't saying much. Then I told him that tomorrow I was going to the store to buy his birthday present, and asked him what he wanted.

He looked up from his cereal and said:

"Everything and a kite."

I was amused at how spontaneous and cute that answer was. I chuckled as I repeated it to myself.

Everything and a kite. That was funny.

I chuckled a second time.

And then I thought, wait a minute. Was that just childlike silliness, or was that the smartest, most calculated answer a four-year-old has ever said?

Think about it!

In the art of haggling, you always ask for more than what you want.

Of course he wants *everything* for his birthday. What kid doesn't? But maybe his thinking was, "OK, I want everything, but just in case Dad tries to talk me down, I'm going to throw a *kite* in on top of that."

Genius.

The more I thought about it, the more I was impressed. It goes beyond genius.

"Everything and a kite" is downright poetic.

We all want the most we can get out of life. But are we ever satisfied? Are we ever content?

No. Something is always missing.

Even if you'd somehow managed to acquire everything you'd ever wanted, you'd still want a little more.

You'd want that kite.

It's human nature.

I think maybe my four-year-old has come up with a new metaphor. We don't want "everything out of life," we want "everything and a kite"!

Son of a bitch, I'm getting a little fired up right now.

I mean, think of how many stupid phrases we say each day that mean the same thing. "The whole enchilada." "The whole nine yards."

That's some weak stuff right there.

"That price includes power steering, CD player, and moonroof. You get the whole nine yards."

Not anymore, chump! You get *"everything and a kite"*!

That's got some flavor, some pop. Matter of fact, if everyone used it once or twice, it could catch on.

I'm not kidding, it could happen.

Get behind it, people! My kid could be the first four-year-old to coin his own phrase. Come on, it's up to you guys. Just try it, that's all I'm asking. Next time you feel you're about to say, "They threw in the kitchen sink," just stand tall and say:

"They gave me *everything and a kite*!"

Yeah, people are going to look at you funny, but so

what? How do you think they looked at the first guy who said "kit and kaboodle"?

No Segues

This is an excerpt from a phone call that I had with my daughter while I was out of town last year. I'm including it to prepare anyone who hasn't experienced a conversation with a six-year-old.

"Daddy, are you going to be home for Halloween?"

"No."

"I have a thousand pennies!"

You got that? No segues.

The Idea for People

Why is the sky blue?

How high is up?

Where do babies come from?

These questions and more, when you join the Parent Club. Act now and we'll send you the thirty-minute "Are We There Yet?" CD, for no extra charge.

OK, don't worry. That's as far as I'm going with this fairly clever but mostly lame parody.

I will say this: of all the questions my kids have asked in my eight years as Dad, there is one that stands out from the rest. It was posed by my daughter when she was five.

"Daddy, how did God get the idea for people?"

It still makes me shake my head.

Not people. The *idea* for people.

What struck me was her ability to cruise past the big issue. Most kids ask, "Who made people?" She knew that. It was God. She'll give you that there's a God.

But how the hell did he come up with *people*? I mean OK, anybody with the title "the Almighty" has to be quick on his feet. But to just come up with people off the top of his head?

Was it his sole idea?

Was there a "ghost-creator"?

Did he have advisers?

It was quite an insightful question for a five-year-old. How did God come up with the idea for people?

What's sad is, "I ask myself the same thing about the Creamsicle."

What's That?

I think we've all experienced the extreme indignity of stepping out of the shower and seeing an empty towel rack.

I'll be honest. I cuss.

Why the towel closet isn't traditionally right in the bathroom itself is a goddamn travesty.

A few years ago there I was, cussing and dripping wet, and on my way out to the hallway of ice.

I flung the bathroom door open and started my dash. Got to the closet when I noticed that down the hall, in front of her room, was my then three-year-old daughter, Alexandra.

Before I could grab a towel and throw it around me, it was apparent from the pointing that she had a question she wanted answered.

"Daddy, what's *that*?"

Please. If there are any architects reading this right now, do you need any more evidence than this to support my theory? How tough is it really? Just get your slide rule, your protractor, erase a few lines, whatever you gotta do, just make it so the towel closet's in the bathroom!!!

Look, I got lucky this time. Before I had to answer, my daughter got distracted by something on TV and ran into her room.

But what about next time, huh? I don't want to be in the "What's that?" situation again.

But if I am, I know what I'm going to say.

"Go get your mother and I'll explain it to both of you."

CHAPTER 11

War Buddies

About ten years ago I remember watching a TV show called *Scared Straight.* It was powerful footage of a social program devised to show wayward kids what the future held for them if they kept going down the wrong path in life. A group of juvenile offenders was taken into a prison to see firsthand the reality of life inside prison walls. Inmates would confront these kids up close and try to scare some sense into them.

In a certain way, I've often thought they should have that same program for couples who have ideas of becoming parents. Just bring them into a room and get them face to face with some real parents, some lifers.

Give them a little taste of reality. Scare the weak ones away. Make sure these punks know what they're getting into before they head down the path to Birth Row.

"Hey, big man! You wanna be a daddy, don't you, tough guy? Hey guys, get a load of Big Daddyboy over here. Man oh man, does he look sweet in those Dockers or what? C'mere, 'Wonder Years,' and let me ask you a question. Think those Dockers are gonna look good with ketchup all over them? LOOK ME IN MY BLOODSHOT EYES WHEN I'M TALKING TO YOU!! That's right, nose to nose. What's the matter, you think I got bad breath? That bothers you? Well, you better get used to it, because that's what happens when a two-year-old FLUSHES YOUR TOOTH-BRUSH DOWN THE TOILET! Who's this? Is this your little wife over here? Oh . . . well lemme get my wife out here. Honey, come here and get a look at this sad momma-wannabe!"

"Oooh. What do we got here? Look at the pretty nails! I guess you got a little of the old 'time to spare.' Well sugar, let's see how pretty your nails look after changing diapers morning, noon, and night. What's that? Nobody's gonna make you do diapers? Let me tell you something, Goldilocks. When that baby comes, you're gonna be nothing but his diaper bitch! So you might be all perfumed and rested now, but do some hard time with Junior, and you're gonna smell like spit-up and fall asleep on the toilet!"

Of course, this would have to be on cable.

I think I've made my point that being a parent is not for the faint of heart. At the end of each day, you need to do your best to recuperate.

There's a moment, after all the yelling and scream-ing and counting to three, when the last kid falls asleep and the house is finally quiet, that it's kind of like a cease-fire in a war.

My wife and I look at each other and know that we've survived another day. We go through the house and slowly count the casualties. A shattered plate of spaghetti and meat sauce on the kitchen floor. Something in crayon on the living room wall. A puddle. I don't know of *what*, but it probably shouldn't be there.

We don't say much to each other as we prepare the battlefield for tomorrow.

We collapse into bed, try to sleep in between nighttime visits from the children, and live to fight another day.

Now, you may have noticed over the last fifty pages I didn't make having children sound all that inviting.

And the reason is simple: that's not the funny angle.

I guess, for the sake of the nonparents, I could try to describe the joy of parenthood, but to tell you the truth, I couldn't do it justice.

CHAPTER 12

Away from Home

I love hotels.

As a comedian, I've done my share of gigs on the road. And yes, traveling has its drawbacks, but I'll say it again:

I love hotels.

I just can't get over how you can leave your hotel room a mess, come back an hour later, and find it's magically clean.

Coming from my house, with four kids, it's just the opposite. Leave a clean room, come back an hour later, and everything's covered in ink. Or something.

There are many little things about a hotel that I used to take for granted before I was married and had children.

For instance, silence.

Ahhh. Hear that? That's a little shot of silence right there. Great, isn't it?

And watch this. If I want to end that silence?

CLICK. ESPN.

Yahoo!

Let's say I'm in a hotel and I want to go to the bathroom uninterrupted. Maybe even read something.

I *can*!

And here's the pièce de résistance, folks. There are some hotels where if you're in the bathroom, and you angle the mirror on the door just right, you can go to the bathroom *and* watch ESPN.

Oh man, just thinking about it . . . I gotta towel off.

Another aspect to the hotel room that you don't get at home is the movies.

The SpectraVision.

And I don't mean *adult* movies, please. Don't try to corner me into that one. I don't partake.

And what if I did?

Does that make me a bad person?

All right! Yeah, I've clicked them on a couple of times! Who hasn't? What's with the cross-examination? Get off my back!

If you must know, I'll never watch one of them again after what happened to me recently. I was being put up in this hotel, all expenses paid. I saw the little card on my TV advertising the adult movies and, as usual, shook my head in disgust.

Then while watching a Discovery Channel special on salamanders, I wavered. I glanced at that little card again. Something seemed strange.

Let me ask you this: Can a card wink?

I also realized that while the salamander program was interesting, I'd seen it before. So I started to think, "What's the big deal? I mean, I'm not interested or anything, but since it's all being paid for, why not turn on one of these things? Just to see what all the hype's about."

So I flicked the TV over to the list of movie categories.

Action
Comedy
Drama
Adult movies
Block adult movies

"Wow!" I thought. "You can get a whole block of them."

Click.

I sat back down and waited. They didn't come on right away. I thought, "Maybe they give people a little time to reconsider."

A little more time passed. Then a little more.

Then a little *more*.

I figured maybe I didn't do it right, so I clicked back on to the category list.

Action
Comedy
Drama

Huh?

Where's the "block adult movies"? I muttered it to myself. The block adult movies.

Block adult movies.

Block adult movies?

Oh my God, I'd BLOCKED THE ADULT MOV-IES!

Is anyone stupider than me?

I didn't know what to do. Could I reverse it? I clicked around . . . no, no . . . I couldn't!

You have to understand the irony here. The whole key to my even attempting this was anonymity. That was the beauty. It's not like I had to go to a video store and rent one. And no one in the hotel knows you're watching.

But now I've got to actually call the front desk and ask them to unblock the porn!

Well, I mean, I didn't *have* to. I could have gone back to the salamanders. But something a little strange was happening.

It seems once you've entertained the initial thought

of watching an adult movie, you've kind of "activated the launch sequence."

Be that as it may, there was no way I was making that call.

So I calmed down. I resigned myself to the fact that the porn would remain blocked.

And then I changed rooms.

While my business traveling lets me stay in hotels, sleep late, and even go golfing sometimes, it's important for me to remember that my wife is home running the household by herself. So, while I may occasionally have fun on the road, I try to keep in mind the most important thing:

Don't let her know it.

And that's a key to keeping the peace between my wife and me. Although it's part of my work, and I'm making money while traveling, I try to leave her with the impression that it's nothing but a burden for me.

Before we had kids that wasn't so important. I could call her while doing a gig on a cruise ship in Barbados and joke around with her.

"Hey, stop your complaining about the subway. You want to talk hot and crowded, you shoulda seen the Jacuzzi."

Now that daily phone call home can be tricky. I've got to downplay any fun.

"Hi, honey."

"Yeah, hi. How's Vegas?"

"Ah . . . you know. Same old . . ."

"You go golfing today?"

"Yeah, but just to be sociable with the other comics. And . . . it was windy."

"Oh, really? I took the kids to my mother's today. Gregory didn't want to get in his seat belt and he started screaming. So of course Matthew started screaming, and they both screamed for the whole ride. I got so frustrated I punched the rearview mirror. It fell off."

". . . . The wind made my lips chapped."

The phone call home is a very delicate task. Here are a few rules I've learned to observe when making it:

1. Never call with the television on.

Don't even try it with the sound off. I used to do that until my wife started catching on.

" . . . and then the baby fell down a well."

"That's nice."

"Bastard."

2. Always let her decide when the call is through.

You have to remember: she's been home all day cleaning asses and feeding faces. Sometimes the opposite. That's some *hard time* she's putting in, and she's entitled to the one phone call, for as long as she wants.

Plus, you gotta let her wrap it up. Don't even try to be cute and steer her into the "let's wrap it up" area with one of those phrases like "Anyway . . ." Because you might just sign yourself up for another fifteen minutes, kicked off by:

"What, I'm boring you?"

3. **Never call right before you have to be somewhere.**

"OK, honey. The show starts in ten minutes, I better get down to the dressing room."

Nobody who's been in a relationship for any length of time falls for this, and not only that, it can backfire on you.

"OK, call me after."

Similarly, never call too early in the day. You're not going to get away with a "talk to you tomorrow" when it's 9:00 in the morning.

4. **Never call during a massage.**

I think that one's self-explanatory.

CHAPTER 13

They Want Your Money

Of all the road gigs I do, Las Vegas is the one that my wife is most sensitive about. Which I understand. It is a wild city. Gambling, nightclubs, showgirls, not to mention legalized prostitution.

You heard me. Legalized prostitution.

I have to be honest: Vegas is my favorite city, not because of any of those things, but being an avid golfer there's a lot of great courses, and you never have to worry about inclement weather.

The only thing that can stop you is the heat. That's my wife's one consolation, that sometimes it's even too hot to golf.

I was there one summer and it was *119 degrees*.

But you know what? I'm from New York. I'd rather be in Vegas when it's 119 than New York when it's 80. And I think you know why.

Legalized prostitution.

In any weather it takes the edge off.*

You know what they say. "It's not the heat, it's the legalized prostitution."

You know Vegas is going to be a little different before the plane even lands. The first time I flew there, I thought the people sitting in the window seats were hallucinating.

"I see a castle! Hey, a pyramid! Oh look, a gigantic lion!"

I thought we were flying over a miniature golf course.

Of course, what those people were seeing were all the new, big, tacky hotels that have gone up over the years. There's always some kind of theme: King Arthur, pirates, McHale's Navy, who the hell knows? Anything and everything.

They've all got a big attraction to pull you in. The Mirage has a replica of an active volcano in the front, and glass-caged white tigers in the lobby.

---

* Normally I don't need to use disclaimers for my jokes, because they all draw on real life experiences. But for this one, let me just say I'm a happily married man and would never solicit the services of a prostitute, except maybe to research a book.**

** OK, normally I don't disclaim my disclaimers, but that, of course, was also a joke.***

*** Hey, what's up?

What the hell does all that have to do with Vegas?

My opinion? Your best bet is to go a few blocks off the strip and find one of the little mom and pop casinos. Something small and quaint and comfortable.

They don't have much. Sure, they try and compete with the Mirage. They've got a white hamster in the lobby. If you need to see an animal, there's your animal. There's no volcano, either. The owner might backfire his truck in the parking lot.

It's not glamorous, but at least the guy at the front desk knows your name.

Listen, big hotel or small, the one thing you find out quick about Las Vegas is they don't mess around.

They want your money.

And they want it quick. You become aware of this as soon as you land and the plane door opens. The first thing you see is a slot machine.

Right there. Ten feet off the plane. I'll tell you, there's no sadder sight than seeing a guy get wiped out before his luggage comes around.

Everywhere you look in Vegas, there's a slot machine. In the supermarkets. I'm not lying. There are slot machines in the supermarkets.

It's pathetic. People with grocery lists in their hands playing video poker, and the more they lose, the shorter the list gets.

"A pair of twos *again*? Well, we don't need eggs."

Oh sure, nowadays they try to make it look like Vegas is a place where you should bring the whole family. There's amusement parks, rides, shows. Something for everyone!

But everything becomes clear when you put your kids on the Ferris wheel, then find out you can bet on them.

And then there's the way they get you in the casinos. Oh, you don't just *walk* in. No, no, no. That would involve letting you go in of your own free will.

They can't take that kind of chance in Vegas. They want to make sure you're coming in. And thus was invented the conveyor belt sidewalk.

"Oh look, honey . . . the sidewalk's moving."

"But, we're not going to this casino."

"Yeah, but it's a free ride."

They're geniuses.

And of course, once you're in . . .

"Honey, we may as well try our luck now that we're here."

You sit down at the blackjack table for a couple hands, she takes one roll of quarters to the slots, and the next thing you know you're looking through the phone book for a place that buys blood.

Now, let's say you're lucky enough to actually win some money, you got a stack of chips in your hands, and you want to collect. You may think you're done playing, but there's one more game ahead of you: find the cashier's window.

And remember, they're geniuses. Guess where you gotta walk to get there? Past every conceivable way to lose more money—craps, slots, baccarat, roulette, a hooker, and a boy with a cup.

Then after you've finally cashed in, I hope you don't think you're going to mosey on out the front door. Because there's a little surprise coming when you get there.

"Hey, wait a minute, the moving sidewalk's only coming *in*!"

What, do you think you're getting a free ride out, you idiot? No, no . . . you want to get out? Do that on your *own* power. And while you're at it, you gotta answer three riddles and cross a rope bridge.

They don't want you to leave. And they'll do whatever it takes to keep you there gambling. They'll wine you, dine you. You want a cigarette? Hey look—cigarette girls! Just walking around the casino floor.

They're my favorites, the cigarette girls. They've got trays of cigarettes, cigars, candy. And other assorted little novelty items.

Yo-yos. Neon yo-yos, for sale on the casino floor.

And I can understand that, because you never know when a high roller is gonna snap.

"Hey, can a guy get a fuckin' yo-yo around here? What's a guy gotta do to get a yo-yo?"

"Take it easy, Frankie."

"No, I won't take it easy. I just dropped fifty thousand, and I'd like to Walk the Dog."

I used to gamble quite a lot when I went to Vegas, but I've since given it up entirely.

I gambled a little too much. Most gamblers have a hard time admitting that. They rationalize. That's the way I was. Every time I'd come home from the racetrack it would be the same story.

"Ma, remember that money you gave me for Grandma's insulin? How about she sweats this week out?"

Gamblers are a funny breed. I read an actual headline in one of the tabloids that read: "Woman Loses Twins in Super Bowl Bet."

As someone who's gambled, I know exactly how something like that could happen.

She probably lost the first twin in the play-offs. Then instead of learning her lesson, she went double or nothing on the Super Bowl.

.   .   .

The first time I quit gambling was a situation most gamblers find themselves in sooner or later: paying off a "promise to God." I was at the racetrack, lost a couple races in a row, and I had quite a bit of money on the next one. So I made a mental promise:

"OK, God. Just let this next horse win and I won't bet again for the rest of the year."

And the horse won.

Which felt great when I was cashing in the tickets. But twenty minutes later when the next race came along, there I was with my racetrack buddy, Bernie, trying to explain my predicament.

"Bernie, you're not going to believe this, but I can't bet anymore. I gotta go home. I made the promise to God."

Of course Bernie, who'd been through this before, told me not to worry.

"Listen, here's what we do. Give me your money, tell me the horse you like, and I'll bet it for you."

Bernie thought he could put one over on *God*.

And as much as he tried to convince me, I didn't buy it. I knew if I put any kind of bet down, God would be watching.

"Is that Romano? Give me the file on him. Look at that—he's breaking his promise! Oh, too bad—I had him winning Lotto next week. OK, gimme a pencil. We'll cross that off. Let's see . . . what do you say we bring back his acne? That'll knock him down a notch. A little acne, and you know what? Give him a slight chest pain. Let him know who's boss up here."

Nothing like a little chest pain to restore your faith.

CHAPTER 14

Food

My last stand-up gig on the road took me to the very beautiful city of Montreal, Canada. I like it there, but here's a little tip if you're ever planning on going:

Learn some French.

They're not crazy about speaking English. It's not like they don't know how, either. Everyone there is bilingual. And I mean everyone. I went into Burger King in Montreal, and the *employees* are required to be bilingual.

Think about that for a second. Burger King. Bilingual.

Have you been to Burger King in this country?

They're not even "lingual."

Don't even attempt language. You're actually better off drawing your food.

"Here. Here's what I want: a hamburger. See? See what I'm drawing? A hamburger. No, put the pie down! I see the pie. I want a *hamburger*! And could I please get it to go? Here, see? I'll draw little feet on my hamburger."

Usually when I go to Burger King, I just take whatever the guy gives me. Even in a worst-case scenario, you're still bringing home a bag of pies.

One of the hassles of the road is having to eat all your meals out, although I don't usually mind it that much. No matter what town I'm in, some restaurant will be serving my favorite meal, soup.

You like soup?

Sure you do.

How could you not? Everybody does. It's too basic a food item to dislike. Saying "I don't like soup" is like saying "I don't care for colors," or "You know what gets annoying? *Music.*"

Soup is unique among foods, because it's tasty, healthy, and everybody can find a type they will like. It's liquid, it's solid, it's hot, it's cold. There's no other food that even comes close. Nothing on God's green earth compares to that magnificent all-encompassing food experience that is soup.

Man oh man, there is nothing like soup.

Well, OK, there's stew.

Stew is kind of like soup.

Actually, it's very close to soup.

———

All right, I stand corrected. I guess there is something that compares.

But you know what? Not to get defensive, but when you think about it, stew actually *is* soup. I mean, come on. It's not fair to put the two into separate categories when the difference is a little extra chewing.

Put it this way: say you're having dinner at someone's house, and you're eating, and you compliment the host by saying, "Wow, this is great soup."

Then the host replies, "Actually, it's stew."

You'd think he was being kind of a dick.

I guess upon further review, I'll revise my position to say, "There's nothing like soup, except stew, which is almost exactly the same."

But all kidding aside, what in the hell is porridge?

From what I understand, and I've read everything about the subject that I can get my hands on, porridge is kind of like a combination of soup and cereal.

Come on.

That's where the cooking people always get into trouble, when they get cute and try to combine foods from completely separate places in the food universe.

Soup and cereal? How did they ever think that was going to work? They're two different species. It's like taping a dandelion to your face and going around saying you're half man, half weed.

And it had to have been invented by accident. No way you're going to be in your kitchen and come up with porridge *on purpose*. No. It's the old two trains colliding and a guy eating clam chowder lands in the lap of a guy eating cornflakes.

Or of course, vice versa.

As you can see, I've got some opinions when it comes to food. Not just soup. I'll cover it all. I can give you my take on anything from, excuse the expression, soup to nuts.

As a matter of fact, let's go to nuts right now.

For my money, and don't argue with me on this, there's no better nut than the pistachio.

Which brings up one of my big gripes about plane travel. You never see pistachio nuts. Oh, you can have all the honey nuts you want. Guess why? They *suck*.

Of course, the honey nut is very plane-friendly. And by that I mean, it's simple. Pick one up, pop it in your mouth, chew.

Which is exactly why pistachio nuts are so much better. They've got to be. For all the work involved in eating one, they better be good.

And by work, I don't just mean the physical labor; I mean the toll it takes on your emotions. There's going to be a lot of ups and downs when you go through a bag of pistachios.

The first couple of nuts, you'll be sailing along with no problems whatsoever. Each nut will have a little slit in the shell. Some will be wider than others. But each shell will have enough of a gap to wedge one of your teeth in and pop it right off.

Ah, the payday when that nut rolls onto your tongue.

One right after the other. You're picking up a little momentum, but then you run smack into a wall.

The completely sealed nut.

Now you have to make some split-second decisions.

Do you bite it, and risk shattering the shell into a million little pieces all over your mouth?

Do you discard it, and live with the feeling of failure for the rest of the bag?

Or do you get a nutcracker, and risk the embarrassment of someone seeing you?

I say you have to go for it. You can't let any nut go by. Some require a little extra work, but what keeps you going is knowing that sooner or later it'll all even out, when you get to one of life's most underrated joys.

The naked nut.

No shell at all. When you get one of the naked pistachios, you feel as if you've just won the nut lottery. There's your reward for all that crap you had to take from the closed guys. And what a reward it is. You can eat the naked nut without one iota of effort.

It's like God said, "Let me get that one for you."

But careful. Keep your wits about you. Don't go getting too happy-go-jacky, because not every naked nut is what it appears to be.

There are impostors. And the cruelest part is, it's not until one of them is halfway down your gullet that you realize you've just swallowed . . .

The *sour* nut.

Mommy.

I have to limit my pistachio intake, because honestly, it's embarrassing to be eating a snack and five minutes later have to call my therapist.

The meal I have the biggest problem with when I travel is breakfast. I don't mean on a plane, I mean breakfast in a restaurant or diner.

I like a glass of juice with my breakfast. A normal-size glass. Have you ordered juice in a restaurant recently? Somebody tell me what's going on in this country. Do we have a shortage? Has Florida put an embargo on us?

Do you know what I'm talking about? Why can't I get a regular-size glass of juice? I'm not asking for much. Twelve ounces, maybe. That's all.

No, no, are you kidding? The only time you're going to see juice in a twelve-ounce glass is when they deliver it to the restaurant.

"Juice delivery! We got your twelve-ounce weekly

juice delivery! Open up the back door, because it's on a hand truck, and we're coming around!"

It's the same thing every time. I tell the waitress I want the large. I specify.

"Please, miss. Your large juice."

You know how it comes?

In a NyQuil cup. That's the large.

If you order the small, they let you suck on a damp rag.

When I was a teenager, I was a waiter for about two years, and I don't remember ever having to ration juice. Of course, a lot of things have changed in waitering.

I worked in a diner, where all the waiters spoke diner language. I don't see waiters do that anymore. I'm sure you know what I'm talking about. For every order of food, we had a certain slang that we would shout out to the cook.

It was creative. It was unique.

Let's say a guy came in and ordered a hamburger to go.

"Kill a cow, and give it shoes!"

In a sense, I considered myself bilingual.

That system really only works in a diner. I found that out when a lady ordered something from me while I was working my next job, at a pharmacy.

"I need some Sominex and some condoms."

"*Sleeping Beauty's got a date!* Anything else, lady?"

"Yes, I, uh . . . I can't really swallow these pills. Do you have suppositories?"

"*The bridge is closed, she's using the tunnel!*"

See what I'm saying?

Makes me kind of sad that you can't go into your local diner and hear that language anymore. Oh, it's still out there.

Sometimes when I'm in a strange town and the hour is getting late, I'll get a yearning to hear it. So I set out for some off-the-beaten-path truck stop where I know it's still spoken.

I stroll in through the double doors, everything falls silent, and all eyes turn to me, as if to say, "Who's the stranger?"

I'll look the place over, and then I'll see him: an old crusty veteran with a waiter's pad in his hand.

He'll look at me, I'll look at him. We won't say anything for a while. There's a little tension in the air. Then:

"What can I do for you, pardner?"

"I'll tell you what you can do for me. You can *send me down the Mississippi in a riverboat*."

At first he doesn't move. No one does. Then a slow smile breaks over his face.

"You want *paddles,* or you *goin' downstream?*"

I usually take a nice dramatic pause, then tilt my head, and in a low contented whisper:

"*Paddles,* brother. *Paddles.*"

Sorry about that. I just saw *Shane.**

---

* Again, don't abuse this language. If you ever order the "going down the Mississippi on a riverboat with paddles," make sure you're in a diner. My friend did it once in a hardware store, and he got stabbed in the neck with a caulking gun.

CHAPTER 15

Driving

When I travel for business now, it's mostly by plane. I have to be honest, I'd rather drive. Or walk.

It's not that I have a phobia about flying, it's that I have a phobia *while* I'm flying. Does that make sense? I'm talking about the sitting during the flying. Not that I mind sitting. Sitting and flying are both fine, it's just that when I sit *while* I'm flying, I . . .

Can I start this chapter over?

All right, I got a little confused. Let's pretend like this is the beginning of the page.

I'd rather drive than fly, because whenever I fly, I'm afraid the person I'm sitting next to is going to want to talk.

There. That's what I was trying to say.

Please understand, I'm a friendly guy. It's not that I'm unsociable. I'm just not a great conversationalist. And nowadays, having to fly a lot between Los Angeles

---

and New York, those long flights can get very tough on a nontalker like myself.

What's made things easier is learning some of the things you can do, tactfully of course, to let the person next to you know you're not the talking type.

First of all, establish this very early.

You can't let any conversation begin. Because once it's started, there's no proper point at which to say, "You've been very nice, but I'd like for both of us to stop talking."

Unfortunately, people interpret many things as an invitation to begin a conversation. It could be anything from eye contact to saying "God bless you" after they sneeze.

So what you have to do is cut off all possible avenues of communication. Your best bet is just to walk on the plane wearing headphones, a surgical mask, and looking through a View-Master.

I know that'll work, because at home, it's the way I go to bed.*

People think I drive only because I'm afraid to fly. That's not it at all. Not only do I know that you are

---

*I make my living through humor. Even so, once in a while my wife will take umbrage at a comment like this that is obviously just a joke. If she does that and wants to talk about it, I will put on headphones, a surgical mask, and look through a View-Master.

statistically more likely to get into an accident in an automobile, but the way my mind works, I worry that while I'm driving, a plane might crash *into my car*.

So I'm going to be neurotic whether I'm driving or flying. As a matter of fact, something happened to me one time on the road that still gives me nightmares. I was driving to a gig, and I noticed a spider on the windshield of my car.

OK, I know that doesn't sound like much of a drama to you, but if you've been reading along, you know I'm not a big bug guy. Yes, you did read that I'm the bug killer, but did you overlook the part where I said they give me the heebie-jeebies?

So there was this big hairy spider right in the middle of my windshield, and all I knew was I wanted him off, pronto. The plan I developed was simple: turn on the wipers and knock him into orbit. For a moment, however, I was torn.

What if all the wipers do is push him a little closer to the driver's-side window? Then what? I think he's gone, I get out of the car, he leaps down my throat and hatches his eggs in my stomach.

Don't laugh! It happened to my friend!

I didn't know what to do. If I had been near a car wash, that might have solved everything, but I was on the highway. Which also ruled out pulling into a garage and getting a new windshield.

I kept one eye on the spider, and one eye on the

road. I couldn't keep that up much longer without getting into an accident. So after a few minutes of trying to "pray" him away, I had to take a chance.

I activated the wipers.

Swish, swish, swish, swish . . .

Nothing. The spider didn't budge.

My cheapo wipers must have been warped, because they were gliding right over the eight-legged beast without moving him a millimeter.

Desperately, I turned on the washer to try and flood him out.

Still nothing.

Then whatever fear I was feeling at the moment was magnified tenfold. I was in my own little horror movie, and I had just gotten a phone call.

"We've traced the spider, Mr. Romano. He's ON THE INSIIIIIIIIDE!"

I'm too embarrassed to tell the end of this story. But here's a hint: moonroof.

Aside from spiders, the only other thing I fear while driving is the dreaded "sleep dip."

Oh man . . . you ever do one of those? Usually they happen late at night, although it's not a rule.

But there you are: behind the wheel of your car, and you're starting to get tired. Your eyelids get a little heavy, and without realizing it, you start to close them just a tiny bit.

Then your head gets a little heavy. Suddenly your chin drops to your chest. The jolt snaps you back awake and your head pops up.

"Wha . . . ? WHOA! Was I just *sleeping*?!"

You can't believe it.

"Oh my God, I was sleeping!"

The first thing you do is look around to see if you killed anybody.

"I think that guy was lying there already . . ."

The sleep dip is not only frightening, it's frustrating. Because how many times are you at home, in your bed, in your pajamas, it's cozy, it's warm, and you can't sleep at all?

Now you're going sixty miles an hour, and you're catching ZZZs behind the wheel.

What amazes me, as frightening as the sleep dip is, is a few minutes after it happens . . . you do it *again*!

You'd think the shock of almost being *killed* would keep you awake for a little while. But no, there goes the old head again . . .

"Wha . . . ? Aw, come on!"

You can't stop it. And it's not from a lack of effort. You try all the tricks to keep yourself awake. You turn on the radio, you open a window, you slap your face. But how in the hell is any of that going to work if almost killing yourself doesn't have an effect?

I'll tell you what I do to stay awake. And I'd appreciate if you kept this to yourself.

I take off my pants.

Underwear and all.

That's right. What, you think I'm weird? I'm a freak? Well maybe so, but it saves lives!

There's no way you're falling asleep like that. No matter what situation you're in, "naked from the waist down" brings a little more focus to it. You develop a Zen-like "oneness" with everything around you. The lights, the wind, the road, the bumps. Especially the bumps.

By the way, I don't mind if you're a little skeptical. I go through that every time I pick up a hitchhiker.

For those of you who frown on nude motoring, let me pass on a real tip, not so much for staying awake, but just to break up the boredom of a long car ride.

Over the years, I've developed a little game that I can play endlessly, whether I'm home, at work, or naked in my car. I guess you could call it a brainteaser, but as you can imagine, if I invented it you don't have to be all that smart to play.

The rules are very simple. As a matter of fact, there's only one:

Come up with a sentence that has never been said before in the entire history of language.

That's it. That's the whole game.

What's that you say? It doesn't sound all that stimulating? Well. Isn't that just great? To me it sounds like you're just not making much of a commitment to the concept.

Get into it! The whole key is this: pretend your life *depends* on coming up with a string of words—not just nonsense, but a real sentence—that hasn't been uttered by anyone, anytime, anywhere.

Just imagine that there's some kind of computer that has a record of every sentence ever spoken. No, I don't know how the computer people could do that. Stop ruining the game with your nit-picking. Just play along.

Come up with a sentence you think no one has ever said.

Let me give you an example.

"Give me back my fudge suitcase!"

Now, I don't know if that sentence has been said before. But we're off to a good start, because I think we can all agree it probably hasn't been said very *often*.

But still, one could probably imagine some kind of situation where "Give me back my fudge suitcase" might have been said in the past. Which brings us to the next phase of the game: once you come up with your "Never Been Said" sentence, you have to try and figure out a scenario where it *could* have been said.

This part is actually the most fun.

"Give me back my fudge suitcase!"

Hmm.

OK, how about this?

Some guy's coming back from Hershey Park, Pennsylvania, and he's loaded up his bags with fudge. He's in the airport, some gung-ho security guy confiscates his luggage . . .

I think you can figure out the rest.

See? See what I'm saying? It's not that easy to come up with a "Never Been Said" phrase.

A lot of times you can find more than one scenario where it might have been spoken. Hell, "Give me back my fudge suitcase" could have been a line from the movie *Willy Wonka and the Chocolate Factory*.

So you see that "Give me back my fudge suitcase" is actually kind of weak.

But here's a tip. Sometimes you can just alter the sentence a little, and that will make all the difference. Check it out:

"Give me back my fudge suitcase, Rockhead."

I think, statistically, we've improved our odds. I mean, how many airport security guards are there named Rockhead, to begin with?

But would you bet your life on it? If you think about it, Rockhead could be what Hershey Man is calling the guard because he's pissed off at him. So you have to take it further.

"Give me back my fudge suitcase, Rockhead Jones and the Five Humidifiers."

OK. I think we may have reached critical mass. If you want to keep going, go ahead, but I'm putting my money on the fact that there was never, ever a musical group named Rockhead Jones and the Five Humidifiers, and even if there was, they never had a fudge suitcase altercation.

Prove me wrong.

To be honest, the most challenging part of the game is to try to keep the sentence short and realistic. Anyone can just keep adding words to the end, but stuff like "Officer Tongue Depressor, could you check under my rumble seat to see if any of the goose-loving woodchucks have cut through my brake line, and also I'm itchy" just gets old after a while. To be honest, it's kind of contrived.

The highest level of competition is to only come up with sentences using things that we know to exist. We know there are no goose-loving woodchucks. And there really is no such thing as a fudge suitcase.

Here's a small list of some of the phrases I've been working on over the years, trying to stay within those rules. Please don't be intimidated by their high quality. You have to understand that while you're just starting out, this is my life's work.

"If hernias were rainbows, I'd be Raymond
Burr."
"Shredded Wheat would make a silly pistol."
"Moonlight is the plumber's pudding."
"My thighs tell the future."
"I'm one headlock short of making colonel."

Not bad, right?
I consider it artistic. Look, I know this type of
thinking is used by musical artists all the time.

"Excuse me while I kiss the sky."

You follow me?
Listen, you might be laughing at me right now, but
next time you're driving in the middle of the night
with nothing to do, you're going to be playing that
game faster than a leg warmer can yell at a helmet.
There's another one for you. That's without even
trying.

In my driving adventures, there's an interesting phenomenon that I've noticed takes place only late at
night. For some reason, otherwise law-abiding citizens
tend to think that the later it is, the less they have to
obey traffic laws at all.
I think you know what I'm talking about.

Driving

It's three-thirty in the morning. You're sitting at a red light. No one's around.

Don't tell me that if it doesn't change within a few seconds, you don't look both ways and roll right through it.

At a certain hour, we all just decide it is now OK to break the law. And you do it without any pretense that it's for a good reason. It's not like your wife's in labor and you're rushing to the hospital.

Literally, the reason you're choosing to break our nation's system of laws is this:

"Come on . . . it's *three-thirty*."

That's it. "It's three-thirty" is the reason. That's what you'd be pleading to a judge if you ever got caught.

"Your Honor . . . it was three-thirty in the morning."

And he'd understand.

"Three-thirty? Why didn't you say so? I'll let you go on that, but what's this in the report about no pants?"

Of course, at three-thirty in the morning, there's really only one motive for not wanting to wait for a light.

You just have to get to Denny's before the weirdos show up.

If you've never been to Denny's, or White Castle, or whatever your neighborhood equivalent is, let me describe what it's like after three-thirty.

It's like a swamp was just let out. People are walking up to the window like zombies.

"Hamburger . . . Hamburger . . ."

You better get there before three-thirty in the morning, or you'll find yourself right in the middle of *Dawn of the Hungry*.

Where I'm from, New York City, the real benefit of driving very late at night is that it's the only time you can find a parking space.

During the day you spend a good chunk of your life trying to find any spot at all. And even if you do find one, you've got to deal with feeding the meter every five seconds.

Sometimes I won't even pull into a spot if there's a meter on it. I'll drive around in hopes of coming across that Holy Grail of parking spaces: the meter with the bag over it.

For those of you who don't know what I'm talking about, in New York City a parking meter with a bag over it means it's broken. It's a free ride for the day.

I've only found one once. It was so exciting. It was close to where I was going, I didn't have to put time on the meter, and I could stay there as long as I wanted.

But when I came back, what I saw reaffirmed was that no one in the world has worse luck than me when it comes to parking.

A cop with a bag over his head, writing me a ticket.

All right, it didn't happen.

Can't a guy stretch reality once in a while for the sake of making his page quota?

And while we're at it, I never drove nude.

New York City drivers have always had a bad reputation. And I'm not going to say it isn't true, but I will tell you what the problem is. It's the testing. It's just way too easy to get a license.

I don't know what the written exam in your part of the country consists of, but it can't be any easier than ours.

Here you go. Sample question.

NEW YORK CITY DRIVER'S LICENSE EXAM

Question 1:

A blind person is crossing the road. What is your
    course of action?

A: *Stop. Let him go by.*

B: *Nudge him a little, so he knows you're there.*

C: *Speed up. Aim for the dog.*

Is this an actual question?

No.

Hee, hee. Page quota.

Actually, I've thought of a very simple solution to the
New York City driving problem. What they should do
is require all drivers to put one of those "How's My
Driving?" stickers with the 800 numbers on their car.

I'm sure you've seen the countless variations of these
on the back of trucks. Some of them are classic. My
favorite one is "How's My Driving? If you have any
complaints, or compliments, call this number . . ."

OK, look: complaints I can see, I can understand
that.

But *compliments*?

Folks, whose life is that boring? Who's making that
phone call?

"Hello, Sternberger Moving Company? I was out on

the road and happened to catch truck number forty-two? He backed into this loading dock . . . it was *artwork*.

"Then, on the way out, he made a U-turn . . . and I wept. Is he ever going to be in town again, because the kids would love him. Listen, I gotta go water my chia pet, but could you put me on his mailing list?"

Of course, you couldn't really have 800 numbers for every car, because the call volume would overload the phone system.

"Hello? I'm leaving you a message because you just cut me off in traffic. Yeah, you're staring at me right now. Looks like you thought it was my fault. Hold on, I'm going to give you the finger. There you go. Ha ha. OK, now we're at a red light. You're getting out of your car, and approaching mine. Tell you what: let me call you back."

CHAPTER 16

Getting Older

The other night, my wife and I had the conversation that made me realize I am now old.

"You want to put the tape in and watch the end of that show?"

"Now? Well, hurry up, it's a quarter to ten."

A quarter to *ten*.

I couldn't believe it. A quarter to *ten* was too late.

Oh my God, when did that happen? I sat back and tried to think how things got this way. When did a quarter to ten turn on me?

As I backtracked through the years, I realized that your perception of "a quarter to ten" correlated to where you were in life.

As a ten-year-old boy, it was exciting. It was a landmark that you bragged about.

"Last night I stayed up until a quarter to ten!"

"Are you kidding? Where was your mother?"

"She drinks."

By the time you've turned twenty, it's lost some of its magic. Now it's too *early*.

"You want to go to that party?"

"Not yet. It's a quarter to ten. Put that tape in, we'll watch the end of that show, and then go."

Then you hit thirty, and a quarter to ten is in limbo.

"Want to go out?"

"Too late."

"Want to go to bed?"

"Too early."

"Want to play Boggle again?"

"OK."

Those are scary times, that limbo era.

Now that I'm forty, a quarter to ten has once again been redefined.

It's late. I'm old.

Some of you may think I'm overreacting.

I got more.

I was at a bachelor party a couple months ago that started out in a restaurant. Happened to end up at a strip club. Don't get me wrong, I didn't suggest it, and nothing bad happened. We were just doing what men do at a strip club: paying seven dollars for a ginger ale, and trying hard not to scream "God Bless America!"

And then, in the middle of the nude mud wrestling, I yawned.

There were naked women. Those women were wrestling. There was mud on them. I *yawned*.

Either I'm old, or I have a whole new chapter to write.

I don't want to sound like I'm whining. I know forty isn't considered that old. But what scares me is that everything in life now seems to be moving by so fast. Seasons pass, and I'm not even aware they came.

What the hell happened to summer? Please, somebody, put a speed bump in the middle of summer.

When I was a kid, it lasted forever! Before lunch, you'd already been in a bike race, fallen out of a tree, found something, tasted it, laughed, cried, pretended you were an assassin, and thrown up.

Now, by the time I realize it is summer, it's Labor Day, and my wife's slapping me because she didn't get a tan.

The days turn into weeks into months into years . . . it just doesn't stop! It's like I'm on the runaway train of life, and all I can do is look out the window and catch the stations as they fly by.

"Christmas!"

"Birthday!"

"Christmas!"

"Birthday!"

"Christmas!"

"Hearing Aid!"

"Dead."

In the blink of an eye, it's all going to be over. And then?

Well, then you enter the afterlife for eternity.

And *that* is gonna drag.

Look, let's say I live until eighty. And that's being generous statistically, but let's go with eighty.

That means, for me at forty, it's *halftime*.

Halftime. Think about that. Half of my life is gone.

I know what I need to do now. I need to do what any great coach does at halftime: go back into the locker room, and get my team ready for the second half.

Shake things up. Little pep talk. Walk up and down the lockers, kick over a chalkboard. Get myself pumped up!

"Pardon my French, ladies, but what the @#$%!! was that? Right from the kickoff it was pathetic. You call that *puberty*? For cryin' out loud, how many times have we gone over this in practice—if you don't lock the bathroom door, your mom's gonna walk in on ya! Then I see you living in your parents' basement, I look up at the scoreboard and it's late in the second quarter! I wanted to grab you by the bell bottoms and yank you off the field right there! Thank God you closed strong with a wife and kids, but let's be honest, that was a Hail Mary play, that works once in a lifetime. Now listen up, idiot. We're within striking distance, but in the second half, if you get all hung up with 'I'm going bald' and 'It hurts when I crap,' next thing you know this game's out of reach! So get out there! Score, and make sure you score *early*. Because we know what happens late in the fourth quarter. You're gonna be walking around with your uniform pulled up to your chest, and we're gonna waste all our time-outs on your hip."

Or something like that.

While I worry about getting older, I have to remember that every age has its anxieties.

Who wouldn't want to be twenty again, right? But if you think back, you realize that twenty has its set of problems too. You still have acne, no one will go out with you, you drive a truck for a mattress company and live in your parents' basement in Queens.

That's just me, but I think the message is universal.

If I could ever really go back in time, I'd go to three years old, no questions asked.

I don't want to bum anyone out, but your happiness peaks at three.

I've lived with three-year-olds, and trust me, you can't be happier.

I was driving to the supermarket once with my

three-year-old daughter, and I'm watching her stare out the back window for fifteen minutes with a smile on her face.

Fifteen minutes, smiling at nothing. There was nothing out there. Finally I turned to her:

"Alexandra, what are you thinking of?"

"Candy."

Candy. *Candy!*

Are you ever happier than that, folks? Don't fool yourself, you're not! When was the last time you daydreamed about candy? Try that when you're forty. Trust me, you don't get far.

"Candy . . . oh . . . cavities. Cavities . . . no money, who am I, why am I here, am I gay?"

There's no room for candy in a forty-year-old's daydream.

I don't daydream much now, although I've noticed as I get older, I do reminisce more. Which isn't a bad thing. There's nothing wrong with reminiscing. Although I actually scared myself the other day. I had just come out of a movie and thought, You know what I miss?

A good quicksand scene.

Now where did that come from? I was reminiscing about *quicksand*. But after thinking it out, it made sense.

All the movies I see nowadays are filled with violence and killing. Look, people get killed in movies, I understand that. But it's how they get killed: all that blood and guts.

You didn't have any of that with quicksand. Yet it was still exciting to watch. As a matter of fact, you had to have an actor in there with some chops, because a quicksand scene ran a gamut of powerful emotions.

There's the panic when you first realize you're in the quicksand. Then there's the screaming and the desperation. Then, determination and the struggling to get out. The reaching for the branch. More sinking and screaming and sinking and screaming and then . . .

Just the hat.

Something strange happens to me when I watch sports now too. I still like watching the game, but there's something weird about knowing I'm older than the Yankees.

Not *the* Yankees, but each individual Yankee.

It's hard to idolize a ballplayer when you're forty and he's, let's say, twenty-one. How can I be yelling "You da man!" when he da *kid*?

What do you know about life when you're twenty-one? That's the difference. When I was a kid watching sports, not only were they athletes, they were my elders. They were inherently wiser.

Now they're still great athletes, but as far as life is concerned, I know more than them.

I remember twenty-one. You think you know it all at twenty-one. Let me put this simply: you don't. All you twenty-one-year-olds reading this, watch as you get older how much more you're going to learn about life.

I'll bet right now you can't even name more than one antidepressant. Go ahead, I'll spot you Prozac.

How can you know about life? You're not even old enough to be neurotic yet.

That's the one thing I have over any twenty-one-year-old: a proud history of accumulated neuroses.

That's the game in which *I'm* da man.

I have to laugh when I see these young kids nowadays, going to therapists with problems like "I'm afraid of commitment."

Don't bring that weak stuff in here.

Grab some pine, rookie, and listen up as Air Romano explains to you how the ocean is plotting against him.

Afraid of commitment? You better bring more than that to your shrink if you want to get into the neurotic World Series with me, pal. Because here's what I bring to mine:

"Why do I cry on Ferris wheels?"

"Are you sure that lump is my wristbone?"

"How do I know everyone who likes me isn't an alien?"

"Is it wrong to have an argument with your legs?"

All right. Maybe I'm exaggerating a little, but trust me, I can take you.

The strongest part of my game is hypochondria.

That's something where age really is an asset. In my twenties, I was like every other guy. I was immortal. Now, every little thing frightens me. Every morning now, I get up and examine myself for something new to worry about. And I always find something.

"Hey . . . what's *this*? Honey, feel this. What the hell is this, right here? I never felt that before. Don't say it's nothing. It's definitely something!"

The only thing that calms me down is when I find that same thing on the other side of my body.

"Oh, wait a minute, it's a *set*, OK, I see. I'm all right. Put the phone down, honey, I'm OK."

The problem with being a hypochondriac is that at this age, my fear of doctors has increased. You'd think you couldn't be any more scared of a doctor than when you were a kid. But as an adult it's worse, because now when you go see the doctor, he has to do some very different things to you.

When you're a kid, he sticks a tongue depressor down your throat, hits your knee with a hammer, and you're done. Nothing worrisome. Nothing, shall we say, *invasive*.

I hope you see where I'm going with this, because here I come. I recently underwent one of the great over-forty rites of passage: my first prostate exam.

I'd never had one, I'd never wanted to have one. But I was forty, and that's the big message. They pound it into you. I saw it on a public service announcement. I saw it in a medical magazine. I saw it in a Hallmark card. "Happy 40th. Bend over."

And as much as I'm a hypochondriac, and I knew I should get it done, I was scared. I was scared of a lot of things. I was scared it was going to hurt.

But I was even more scared that it *wouldn't*.

And let me tell you something: the night before a prostate exam is quite a learning experience. According to the nurse—and for this next line I wish there was a font for *shame*—I had to perform an enema on myself.

At first I thought they were kidding. Didn't I have enough to worry about? I was ready to cancel because I had already used up all of my "just-get-through-it-you'll-be-happy-you-did-it" rationalizing on just the exam.

But I didn't cancel. A weaker man might have. And to tell the truth, it wasn't as bad as I thought. I got through everything just fine. Oddly enough, the most uncomfortable part about the whole ordeal was after the exam, in the doctor's office, when he turned to me and casually said:

"You did a great job with your enema."

OK, now listen, I'm the first to admit that I have a hard time accepting compliments. I get a little bashful. But you have to admit, in this case I had a right to be a little tongue-tied.

And while I fumbled for something to say to him, he trumped himself with a follow-up question.

"Who helped you with it?"

Who *helped* me with it?

I'm going to take a minute now, just for that to soak in for you folks. The question being posed to me was: Who helped me with my enema?

Now, I don't know, maybe it's a legitimate question. Maybe in doctors' circles, that's small talk. But to me it just seemed wrong.

"Who helped you with your enema?"

First of all, how many possible answers to that question are there? How long a list of people could that be?

"You know, it's funny you ask, Doc. I was home alone, and then the mailman came by. We got to talking . . ."

What did he want me to say? The answer is, *nobody* helped me!

My question is, WHY DID HE HAVE TO *KNOW*? Was he that impressed? Is that what it was?

Because when you think about it, he didn't ask, "*Did* someone help you?" He went right to "*Who* helped you?"

He was *that* sure this was a two-person job. I was afraid to tell him it was just me, because maybe he'd think I was insulting his ability to appraise such a thing.

"You're not going to sit here and tell me that was all *you* down there. I've been in this business forty-five years, and you're gonna tell me that *nobody helped you with that perfect enema?* Get out of my office!"

I left there thinking two things. I'm in pretty good health, and maybe I missed my calling.

One of the good things about getting older is that you lose your memory, so soon I'll forget the whole incident.

Actually, my memory loss is becoming more and more prominent now. I'm forgetting things I never thought possible. My own phone number.

Is that normal? I *forgot my own phone number*. It's actually very frightening, to be talking to someone: "Yeah, give me a call, I'm at 4-5-7- . . . uh, OK, hold it. It's 4-5-7- . . . OK, what's going on here?"

It's hard to believe. And then you try to say it faster, thinking that'll give your brain a running start.

"Here we go. Ready? 4-5-7- . . . aw, come on!"

This is why businesses use words for phone numbers. And even though it helps you remember, I hate it because it takes me twenty minutes to figure out how to dial 1-800-CAT-FOOD.

What's worse is when people try that system for their own numbers.

"Yeah, give me a call. I'm at 5-KLON-42."

Nobody's going to remember that. Then they offer to help you out.

"Hey, did you know that your number spells out JL5-PINI?"

You ever have this memory loss? You're in your shower, you're daydreaming, and you can't remember if you *shampooed your hair*?

Oh, that scared the hell out of me. You have to backtrack in your own shower.

"Hmmm, let me see . . . my hair feels squeaky . . ."

You know what I do now? I just bring a checklist right into the shower. Then I check each thing off after it's done.

- ✓ Turn on cold water
- ✓ Turn on hot water
- ✓ Burn
- ✓ Freeze

- ✓ Burn, but a little less
- ✓ Wash
- ✓ Lather
- ✓ Sing "Piano Man"
- ✓ Rinse
- ✓ Check for ticks

That's pretty much it.

Well, not everything. There is something that isn't on the list that I occasionally do in the shower, but I'd really rather not discuss it.

I think the men know what I'm talking about.

Thaaaaaaaaaaaaaaat's right.

It's nothing to be ashamed of. It's healthy. God gave us a gift, and look, sometimes in the shower we use it.

What's funny is that sometimes we have no intention of doing that at all, and you even tell yourself that as you're going in.

"Look, I'm late. I'm just gonna wash it and be on my way."

Then you get in there, and the next thing you know, you're trying to seduce *yourself*.

"Relax. I know we're late. I just wanna hold it, that's all."

There's a reason why men engage in that activity much more than women. It's not our fault. We were given the power of fantasy. I know women fantasize, but ladies, you have no idea what men are mentally capable of.

It comes with being a man. It's like when you buy a computer now, and it comes with Windows. Same theory applies. We're preloaded.

We have a cast of thousands in our heads. It's ridiculous. There's too many! There's people in there you don't even want half the time.

"What are you doing here, Mom?! Get out! Security, my mother's in here!"

I don't know about you, but when my mother makes a cameo, show's over.

What men really need is a director. Right there in our fantasies. Someone who can keep the show running.

"OK, everybody, come on, gather 'round, he's in the shower! Show time. Look alive. We have a new cast member today. Hi. You want to introduce yourself?"

"I'm Julie."

"Well, welcome to the crew, Julie. Nice to have you aboard. So how did you get here?"

"He saw me bend down in the subway."

"Yeah, yeah . . . we get a lot of people that way. Now, don't be nervous, and just remember one thing: the better you are, the quicker we're all out of here. OK? So let's give him a good show. By the way, are you bisexual?"

"No."

"Well, you are now."

Throughout this chapter, it may have seemed as though I'm constantly miserable about my age. But don't worry about me. I'm pretty much content with where I am and what I've got.

And whenever I do get down about life going by too quickly, what helps me is a little mantra that I frequently repeat to myself.

"At least I'm not a fruit fly."

Does that need more?

What it means is, I think of how lucky I am that I don't have the life span of a fruit fly: one day.

One *day*.

Now that's pressure. You're born, and by lunchtime you're having a midlife crisis. And if you die before lunch, it's a tragedy.

"Oh, how sad . . . he had his whole *day* ahead of him."

I have to consider myself lucky. I mean, just imagine that—a one-day life span? What if it's a day that sucks? What if you gotta go help another fruit fly move? Or pick him up at the airport? Maybe you gotta wait around all day for the cable fly to come over.

I don't even know why God would create a species

that only lives one day, unless it was to make the gold-fish feel good about himself.

"Look, we're goldfish. We're gonna be dead in a week, but that's seven times longer than a fruit fly."

While repeating my mantra does make me feel better, it's not long until I sabotage it by also repeating:

"I'm not a sea turtle."

Does that need more?

The sea turtle lives to be two hundred. I did a little figuring. If I were a sea turtle, I'd be the equivalent of fifteen.

Of course, I take a little solace in knowing that you can't just weigh how long you live, you've got to factor in quality of life.

As a matter of fact, given the choice of being a fruit fly or a sea turtle, my pick might surprise you.

Let's break it down.

As a sea turtle, you'd live until two hundred. But here's the particulars:

Your home is your shell, so you can never leave the house. You can eat anything you want, but all your food is faster than you. And let's not forget, if you get flipped on your back, it's over.

Now here's the fruit fly life:

Reproduce.

That's it. For their entire one-day life, they reproduce. So maybe there is some poetic justice to God's plan after all.

"Look, fruit flies: you're going to live one day, but listen to the day I have planned!"

You know what? Knowing all the details, I might just go with being a fruit fly.

Of course, I know what would happen. I'd be a creature whose only purpose in life is to reproduce, and I still wouldn't be able to score.

That'd be the story of my one-day life: propositioning a female fruit fly and hearing:

"Maybe tomorrow."

CHAPTER 17

Anna's Chapter

Wow. The book's over.

I'm pretty spent.

I don't know about you, but I could use a backrub and a good swift kick in the ass.

But that's just me. You?

You just accept my gratitude for reading the whole thing. At least I can take solace in knowing that if you've read this far, it must have been pretty good.

Then again, you could have just read a little of every chapter and said, "I'm gonna skip to the next one because this one is BORRRRRRRRRRRRRRRRING."

I think I've said a lot in this book. Quite a few things that are very personal.

I guess I've talked about my wife the most. Which makes me feel a little guilty. Let's face it, I talk about her all the time in my stand-up, and now I'm writing about her in my book. There's really no venue for her to rebut what I'm saying.

Then I thought about letting her write this final chapter. That's right, actually giving her a few pages to let her say how she feels about me.

But then I had another thought:

"No."

I came to the conclusion that it might be asking for trouble. Besides, what the hell? This is a book, not a *debate*.

Instead I thought, "You know what? Since I have a hard time telling it to her face, I'll use these last few pages of the book to express how much I appreciate her."

Boy, I hope she's buying this.

I seldom put into words the many things I love about my wife. And since she's probably reading this right now, mouthing the words "Spare me," I'll get specific.

I love her laugh, her sense of humor, her kindness, how great a mother she is. But most importantly, what I love in her is *truth*.

The truth we have with each other.

That's been very special to me since we first met, but even more so now that I have a TV show and a book and whatever small amount of so-called fame. It's always there, the truth. Her unaffected true feelings for me.

I thank God that my wife is with me on this little

ride that I'm taking, because it keeps me from ever losing perspective.

I think the best example of what I'm talking about is a phone conversation I had with her after I first went out to California. She was still in New York with the family.

It was the day after the premiere of my show, and to celebrate, the network was taking my friend and me to Vegas.

I could hear a little sarcasm in her voice when she told me to "have a good time," so I decided to play around with her and give her some big-shot show business attitude.

"Hey, I don't want any lip from you, sweet sister! I don't know if you know who you're talking to, but this here is a man whose show just premiered on a major network. Catching the magnitude of that? Millions of people sat down in front of their TV sets last night for a half hour, just to watch yours truly."

To which my wife replied:

"You're still the dick I married."

And that's it right there. That's what I need from her, and I get it. The purity, the clarity, the truth.

"You're still the dick I married."

That's what I have to remember, no matter where this road takes me. Because you know what?

I am.

Special Thanks

This page right here, the words you're reading right now, are the only ones I wrote in this book without the help of two very talented people, Brad Kesden and Mike Royce.

Brad Kesden not only had to sit and listen to me tell boring stories about my life, and then watch every boring video of me that ever existed, he had to show me how to turn it all into a funny book. Until he was introduced to me, I didn't believe I could write one. His professional and comedic participation made it all possible.

Mike Royce, my comedy-writer friend from New York, suffered cruel and unusual punishment. Although his wife, Jennifer, was six and a half months pregnant with their first child, I dragged him to Los Angeles, locked him in my office, and forced him to help me for seven weeks. That was the price he had to pay for being able to write comedy exactly the way I would. I felt justified with the abduction because his sensibility and style were just so perfect for my book. Besides, I gave him pie.

I thank both these men. They saw me at war with the Battle of the Blank Page and joined me on the front lines.

(If that last analogy sounds lame, it's because, like I told you, I wrote it myself. . . .)

Acknowledgments

When it comes to this book, there are so many nice people to whom I owe thanks for all their help. I think you know who you are, but let me refresh your memory:

Rory Rosegarten, my manager and friend from the very beginning;

Everyone at The Conversation Company Ltd.;

Mel Berger and James Dixon at William Morris;

Irwyn Applebaum and the Bantam gang;

Jon Moonves; Jon Moonves's brother, Les; my great assistant, Valerie Dekeyser;

All the wonderful people at the production office of *Everybody Loves Raymond;*

Jennifer Royce for lending me her husband;

And of course, my wife and kids, who, now that this book is completed, I look forward to getting to know again.